Praise for *Vocal Intelli*

How can we tap our voices to strengthen our leadership, relationships, and well-being? This delightful and trustworthy guide will support us in developing our voices in this way—and offers us encouragement and inspiration as we learn.

—Margaret Wheatley, author of thirteen books from *Leadership and the New Science* to *Restoring Sanity*

This book opens a new pathway into personal healing. It offers a means to reconstruct our story about ourselves and our presence in the world. Barbara McAfee calls this practice *vocal intelligence*. This is a groundbreaking piece of work in both its concept and its invitation to engage. —Peter Block, author

I am a longtime fan of everything Barbara McAfee does. I love the wise, practical, and innovative ways she invites leaders to find their voices. If you are called to lend your voice and leadership to creating a more harmonious world, you will find this book an essential companion.

—Parker J. Palmer, author of *Let Your Life Speak, A Hidden Wholeness,* and *Healing the Heart of Democracy*

Barbara's calling is your voice. In ways practical, expert, skilled, and soulful, she will help you realize, share, and enjoy the fullness of your voice. You will live more fully as you grow from her invitation to full vocal expression.

—David O Fallon, PhD
Former president, MacPhail Center for Music
and former president, Minnesota Humanities Center

This book is the perfect medium for Barbara McAfee's brilliance to shine through. She has taught thousands to discover the "story of their voice," and you will absolutely find yours—and much more—as you read her profound lessons on vocal intelligence.

—Jennifer B. Kahnweiler, PhD, CSP
Author, *The Introverted Leader: Building on Your Quiet Strength*

In this creative and practical book, Barbara challenges us to find our voices and think deeply about how they reflect and support our calling. This profound work connects us to one of our most basic human needs: finding our authentic voice and expressing our authentic selves.

—Nick Nissley
President, Northwestern Michigan College

Barbara McAfee shows leaders the power of discovering their full voice. Her vision is compelling: our voices can embody the qualities we most want to bring to ourselves and our teams. She's discovered how to apply a growth mindset to the voice and shows how anyone can shape their voice through deliberate practice.

—Kevin Majeres, MD
Cofounder, OptimalWork
Psychiatrist, Harvard Medical School

This book is the perfect place for Barbara McAfee to share all that she has been learning and discovering these past thirty years of working with the human voice. My teacher's teacher, Alfred Wolfsohn, once said, "The voice is the muscle of the soul." I believe that Barbara embodies that saying in all that she teaches.

—Saule Ryan

Teacher/actor, The Roy Hart Centre, Malérargues, France

In a world where authentic connection is vital, Barbara masterfully reveals how our voices can express and shape our identity. An essential read for anyone seeking to harness sound's transformative power personally and professionally.

—Quanita Roberson

Author, storyteller, life coach, and international public speaker

A wisdom singer has arrived carrying a book that can enrich lives, strengthen effectiveness, deepen relationships, open vistas to new possibilities, heal ancient wounds, restore courage, incite sweet laughter, and make the whole world happier. And all in the name of the Voice. Thank you, Barbara. You deserve a great praise song for this exemplary work.

—Peggy Rubin, director,

Center for Sacred Theatre; author, *To Be and How To Be*

Leading with *Vitality, Presence,* and *Impact*

BARBARA McAFEE

Published 2026 by Gildan Media LLC
aka G&D Media
www.GandDmedia.com

Front cover design by David Rheinhardt of Pyrographx

Interior design by Meghan Day Healey of Story Horse, LLC

Library of Congress Cataloging-in-Publication Data is available upon request

ISBN: 978-1-7225-0738-1

10 9 8 7 6 5 4 3 2 1

For Saule Ryan

Teacher, colleague, and beloved friend:

Who would I be without you?

CONTENTS

{PART THREE}
Who Are You Going to Be While You Do What You Do?

INTRODUCTION

Something called you to this book.

Out of all the possibilities, you chose this one. I wonder why.

Perhaps you have a hunch that your voice is central to your success.

Maybe you've heard a recording of yourself and cringed. Or you recently received feedback that stung. Perhaps your voice failed you in a moment that mattered—or you struggle to make yourself understood.

Or maybe, just maybe, you followed a yearning you can't quite name.

Whatever brought you here, I'm glad you came.

At the heart of this book is a single, powerful question: *Who are you going to be while you do what you do?*

There is a profound connection between your voice and the work you're called to do in the world. The Latin verb *vocare* means *to call, invoke*, or *name*. From it, we get words like:

Vocation: our work in the world
Avocation: what we love to do
Advocacy: speaking on behalf of what matters
Provocation: shaking things up

And my personal favorite:
Invocation: calling the sacred into the world with our voices

Leadership amplifies everything we do. Whether you hold a formal title or simply step up when it matters, your voice carries weight. Your tone, your timing, your ability to speak and listen—all of it shapes the world around you.

We've all heard plenty about emotional intelligence: the capacity to understand feelings and connect deeply with ourselves and others.

But what about *vocal intelligence*?

It's not enough to simply know the emotional terrain. We also need the skill to express our emotions through the sound of our voices.

Vocal intelligence is the bridge between thinking, feeling, and communicating. It lets our voices carry warmth, clarity, conviction, or tenderness. It's how we help others feel safe, inspired, or understood.

It's one thing to think and feel deeply. It's another to give those thoughts and feelings shape and sound. That's the power of vocal intelligence.

Much of leadership is made of conversation. The best leaders communicate with intention, flexibility, and skill. They listen deeply, invite others' voices, and respond to what they hear. This call-and-response builds cultures of trust and resilience. If you've experienced that kind of leadership, you know what a gift it is.

Voice is foundational. Every organization began because someone gave voice to an idea. Every team, every relationship, every mission relies on conversations that move things forward. And yet few of us were ever taught how to use our voices well.

In my twelve years as an organizational consultant, the top challenge named by every team—without exception—was communication. Often, the breakdown wasn't about systems or platforms, but about how people *sounded* to each other. Misunderstandings arose from tone, body language, and facial expression. As tensions rose, people doubled down on styles that weren't working. Trust eroded. Conversations collapsed. Repair took time, patience, and the willingness to listen anew. Over and over, I saw how profoundly voice shaped both the fracture and the healing.

Consider the many ways you use your voice in a single week:

Presenting to a group.

Coaching a colleague.

Inspiring a client.

Some of these interactions happen face-to-face, others virtually. Each requires a different kind of vocal presence. Yet most people move through all of them without much awareness.

Now here's something deeper: your voice mirrors your identity. It tells a story about who you believe yourself to be, even when you're not conscious of it. As your vocal range and flexibility grow, so does your sense of possibility. You can't change your voice without your life coming along for the ride.

My intention for this book is simple: to change the way you think about and use your voice—every single day. This journey will be surprising:

You'll awaken to the role voice plays in your daily life.

You'll be invited to make some unexpected sounds using the Five Elements Framework™, a model I created to help access more flexibility, vitality, and impact in the voice.

You'll experiment with each element, uncovering your own vocal strengths and challenges and how they play out in your leadership.

I'll also share stories of leaders who have transformed their work by transforming their voice.

You'll become a sharper listener.

You may even reclaim lost parts of yourself in the process.

Finally, we'll gather practices to help you sustain your energy and humanity as you lead in this changing world.

Before we begin, I want to share a story that captures the kind of leadership I hope this work will foster.

I'm standing on the TEDx stage before 1,000 people in Bend, Oregon. I teach them a four-line song: call and response. Once they have it, I tell them the plan: when we start singing together, I won't decide when we stop. *They* will.

I've done this experiment many times, with fifty, 100, even 300 people. And somehow, each group always lands on a collective decision. No conductor. No cue. Just a shared knowing. But 1,000 people? I'm not sure it'll work.

We begin singing a simple four-line song. My friend plays a drum quietly to support, not lead. Harmonies rise. The room shimmers. Then a shift. I feel it. The group is ready. The volume drops. And then: silence. All at once. Unplanned. Perfect.

The silence is luminous. Alive. Then the room erupts with applause and wonder. How did we do that? How indeed?

This is the kind of leadership I want to cultivate: not control, but invitation. Not perfection, but resonance. A field where collective genius can emerge.

I'm not here to turn you into a conductor or a song leader. I am here to help you awaken the full power of your voice so you can listen, respond, and lead with clarity, courage, and connection.

Let's begin.

{PART ONE}

The Voice, Hidden in Plain Sight

EXPLORING YOUR VOCAL STORY

Now let's open a deeper, broader inquiry into voice.

I'd like to begin by offering you a question.

Take a moment to pause and make a note—in your journal, a voice memo, or just in your mind—of what comes up when you read it.

Ready?

What is your story about your voice?

This is the question I use to open nearly every session, every workshop, every training I lead. I've asked it of thousands of people over the years.

Here are the most common responses I hear. Maybe some of them will resonate with you:

1. **"I've never thought about it."**

This is by far the most common response. Isn't it curious? Something we use constantly in work, parenting, community, and leadership, and we rarely consider its story, its history, or its potential.

If you've ever lost your voice to laryngitis or some other illness, you know how essential it is.

And we are always responding to the voices of others, consciously or not.

It is strange that voice stays so invisible, so unexamined.

2. **"There's something wrong with it."**

Once in a while, someone tells me they love their voice—and I celebrate that along with them. But most often, I hear complaints:

"My voice is too nasal."

"I sound too young."

"It's too monotone."

"I talk way too fast."

"My voice gets hoarse all the time."

"I can't be heard in noisy places."

And almost everyone says, "I hate the sound of my voice when I hear it recorded."

Let me tell you the reason for that one. It all has to do with physics. When you hear your voice inside your head, the sound is conducted through *bone*. Out in the world, it's conducted through *air*. The difference in sound makes sense when you consider the difference between the density of bone and air, yes?

But what interests me most is not the physics: it's the intensity of our discomfort.

We're not just reacting to an odd sound. We are overwhelmed by the gap between our own perception and what other people are hearing. When we say, with utter horror, "Wait, is that *me*?" it's a clear sign of how deeply voice and identity are entangled.

3. **"Something happened to me in childhood."**

This is where the tenderness comes in. I've heard so many heartbreaking stories about how trauma, abuse, secrecy, and shame can take root in the voice, causing it to shrink, retreat, or even go silent.

Sometimes the voice gets quieter. Sometimes it gets louder and sharper out of a need for self-protection.

But either way, the voice absorbs the trauma.

4. **"I'm terrified to speak in front of people."**

Fear of public speaking—glossophobia—ranks just below the fear of death on many lists.

It's no wonder, given the miserable experience it is! The pounding heart, shaking knees, pouring sweat, and racing thoughts are bad enough without the anticipatory dread beforehand and the cringing shame afterwards.

I know this fear intimately. I've lived it. And I've walked with hundreds of people as they slowly, bravely found their way through it.

This fear is rarely just about performance. It's what happens when we confront our visibility, vulnerability, and power—and the resulting cascade of physical and emotional turbulence.

5. **"I was told I couldn't sing."**

I am constantly astonished at the number of people who stopped singing because of one offhand comment from a teacher, parent, sibling, or friend. It's a staggering loss.

It often happens in childhood, in a moment of careless critique:

"You're off-key."

"Maybe just mouth the words."

"You're not a singer."

Just like that, the door closes.

But here's the truth: most people are not nearly as bad at singing as they believe.

And even if they were, so what?

You have an innate right to sing, even if no one ever hears you. Singing is your birthright: a gift handed down from your singing ancestors.

Wherever you are from in the world, know that your ancestors sang. They sang to honor the seasons, lend rhythm to their work, educate the young ones, and invoke the sacred.

That singing is one reason they endured the unendurable and made it possible for you to be here now.

6. **"My voice disappears."**

Some people lose their voice physically from overuse or illness. Others lose it situationally: in meetings, under pressure, or with authority figures. Suddenly their voice becomes soft. Meek. Flat. Or it disappears altogether.

This isn't a technical issue. It's grounded in relational, emotional, and historical blocks.

7. **"I want to find my voice."**

This one is more metaphorical, but no less real. Many people carry a longing to be fully expressed, to feel their voice rise up unencumbered by fear or tension, to let their gifts move through them and out into the world.

I believe this longing is sacred. And I believe the world needs what only *your* voice can offer.

If you want to go deeper, try writing, or recording, a vocal autobiography.

Begin by reflecting on these questions:

If your voice could speak its own story today, what would it say to you?

What would you say in return?

Then gently explore these questions:

What are your earliest memories of speaking or singing—the joyful ones and the painful ones?

What turning points shaped your voice? Were there moments of pride, loss, growth, or silence?

When you imagine your voice set free, what images, feelings, or dreams arise?

Now that you've taken a look at your story about your voice, let's deepen our exploration of the connection between voice and identity.

2

VOICE AND IDENTITY

Let's begin with another etymological invitation.

The word *persona* comes from the Latin *personare*, meaning *to sound through*. It referred to the mask worn by actors in early Roman theater that amplified the voice.

Our voice is like a kind of amplifier: a sonic projection of the story we've come to believe about who we are.

But voice is more than sound. It's breath, body, vibration. It's the living mirror of everything you've lived through and everything that has shaped your sense of self.

Your persona, your self-story, was forged over time. Through family. Culture. Relationships. Success. Pain.

This process is like echolocation, the way bats navigate in the dark. They send out tiny clicks and map their world by listening to the echoes.

You did something similar. As a baby, you sent out cries, giggles, coos, and whimpers—each one a tiny risk, a vocal experiment. What echoed back from the people around you—comfort or neglect, delight or disapproval—shaped your earliest maps of safety and belonging. That echoing continued with siblings, teachers, peers, and strangers. You learned which sounds brought connection and which ones brought trouble.

Meanwhile, you were soaking in other messages, from media, advertising, social scripts, that whispered (or shouted):

"Be louder."

"Something's wrong with you."

"Be smaller."

"Be like her or him."

"Be quiet."

"You need fixing."

"Change who you are."

Many of these messages were not only unrealistic but manipulative, designed to exploit your doubt in order to sell you something.

Later, new frames came along: personality assessment tools such as Myers-Briggs, DiSC, the enneagram, and CliftonStrengths. These tools can be helpful mirrors, but they can also become boxes. Labels. Self-concepts that harden into cages.

Over time, you may have made up your mind about what kind of person you are—and what kind you are *not*—based not on the truth of your nature, but on a mishmash of echoes, assessments, and assumptions.

But here's the thing: every time you speak, your voice tells the story.

It reveals where you're open.

Where you've armored up.

Where you've surrendered.

And where you're still fighting for your full humanity.

Just by hearing the sound of your voice, others can sense your age, gender, emotional state, health, education level, and region of origin.

You might think you're being guarded, but your voice doesn't care about privacy settings. It tells the truth. Sometimes in ways that you'd find disturbing.

Still, most of us barely notice our voices or assume what we have now is all there is. We think, "I guess this is just how I sound."

But that's a myth.

Your current voice is not the whole house: it's a broom closet. Inside you is a mansion of sound, nuance, possibility, and power.

I'm inviting you to open the door—to open up your full voice with all of its gifts and mysteries.

Because voice is not just personal or professional. It's also relational, spiritual, and even transformational. Your voice holds more than your story; it holds your becoming.

Here is what I want you to know, not just in your mind, but in your bones:

You are more than your story.

You are more alive, more creative, more resilient, and more brilliant than you've ever been led to believe.

And your voice holds one of the keys to unlocking that radiant, resonant potential.

Opening up more of your sound can also stir up some old ghosts and fears. Let's take a peek into the shadow and how it dances with your voice.

3

VOICE AND SHADOW, OR, WHAT'S IN YOUR BASEMENT?

Your voice is connected to your deepest instincts. Changing it from the inside out is not just a technical act: it's a courageous one. This book isn't simply about vocal tips and tricks, although you'll pick up a few of those along the way.

The most powerful shifts come when your voice is infused with physical vitality, emotional truth, full-bodied breath, and clear intention. Taking that risk—being seen and heard in your wholeness—often awakens parts of you that have been dormant or exiled.

Soon I'll be inviting you to make sounds that stretch your entire vocal range. Most people find this process physically enlivening, emotionally liberating, sometimes even joyful.

But let me give you a heads-up. Some of the sounds will be uncomfortable. Maybe even irritating.

Here is something else you should know: the vocal qualities you like the least often hold the greatest gifts. In my experience, these sounds often bump up against the parts of ourselves we've worked hardest to suppress: rage, shame, lust, greed, jealousy. You know, the seven deadly sins . . . plus a few extras.

We learn early on that these feelings are "too much." As children, we are shushed, shamed, punished. Sometimes the lesson goes so deep that it shapes our very ability to make sound.

One individual trained in my work shared a story that still haunts me. She grew up hearing constant messages to always talk pretty, sing pretty, *be* pretty. It became so ingrained that she gave birth to two full-term babies in complete silence, with no medication.

I've never birthed a child myself, but I've been present at several births. I've even trained expectant parents in how to use sound to help them through labor. I cannot imagine how she managed to stay silent through such a primal, intense act.

Through tears, she confessed that this story gave her a sudden, painful glimpse into how her family's dynamics had completely shut down her voice.

Those tears turned into laughter and relief when I invited her to reclaim those long-suppressed sounds. Even though her children are grown up now, the guttural, powerful birth songs were still there, waiting to be expressed.

The voice remembers. It's ready to return at the slightest invitation.

When you open your voice to new territories, it may stir up fear. You may hear a voice in your head saying things like:

"You look foolish!"

"That's a bit much, don't you think?"

"You should be seen and not heard!"

"Oh, boy, you're going to get in trouble . . ."

One reason for these objections is that you may be expressing your shadow.

The founder of analytical psychology, C.G. Jung, defined the shadow as the unconscious, repressed aspects of the personality that we find undesirable or socially unacceptable. He taught that what we resist persists. Nowhere is this more apparent than in our voices.

Our shadow isn't hiding in some back room of the psyche; it's humming under our breath, leaking out in sarcasm, hesitation, tension, or an unexplained loss of words.

Once we step into leadership, the stakes only rise. We can't afford to be too angry, too emotional, too loud, too soft, too needy, too anything.

So the shadow gets pushed down, locked in the basement.

But here's the truth: The shadow doesn't go away. It just waits. When ignored for too long, it erupts.

It might sneak out when someone cuts you off in traffic, when your teenager says something cruel, when you're running on empty and snap over something tiny. Suddenly the basement door flies open, and out it comes—fangs, warts, glitter, and all.

As leaders, we're called not only to deal with our own shadows but also to navigate the shadows of those we lead. Yet many of us lack healthy outlets for expressing the shadow. We spend our workdays being responsible and smart. Then we go home and try to model good behavior for our families. We often take on visible roles in our communities that call us into our best selves.

So where do we cut loose, act out, misbehave a little? Where's the room in our well-ordered lives for the shadow to have its say?

Some people let loose by riding motorcycles, practicing martial arts, attending sporting events, or going wilderness camping. More often, though, the shadow erupts when we're triggered, stressed, or exhausted, and *wham*! We're yelling, sulking, or hiding under the covers, thinking dark thoughts.

Our shadows will find a way to express themselves, no matter what. If we don't give them voice on purpose, they'll work mischief in our lives, often leading to illness, conflict, depression, or addiction.

Let's be honest. Humans need breaks from being good, from acting smart, from holding it all together. We need sanctioned moments to get rowdy, weird, messy. We need to misbehave—safely, creatively, and collectively. That's not regression; it's renewal.

In her beautiful book *Dancing in the Streets: A History of Collective Joy*, Barbara Ehrenreich describes how human cultures once offered frequent opportunities for people to cut loose through celebrations, dancing, feasting, and general revelry. These rituals gave us a break from individuality and let us fall into the collective. They provided safe, socially sanctioned outlets for expressing the shadow.

Some of these traditions remain, in carnival, Mardi Gras, big sporting events, and rock concerts, but they're far fewer than in our ancestors' time. Ehrenreich traces the disappearance of these communal wild spaces to a rise in what was then called *melancholia*. Without wildness, we fall into depression.

Many of the sounds and characters we explore in the Five Elements Framework run directly counter to cultural norms. Inhabiting these characters gives us space to be animalistic, brash, mushy, shrill, flighty, seductive—all the things polite society frowns on—and to do it in ways that are playful, harmless, and often healing.

So, as you begin practicing the exaggerated sounds in the coming chapters, allow yourself to stretch beyond the bounds of your usual character and behavior.

Go ahead and give voice to your snarky teenager.

Guffaw like a boneheaded dolt.

Throw a temper tantrum like an outraged toddler.

Simper and sigh like an airhead.

By letting your shadow have a voice, you may reintegrate vital aspects of yourself that you surrendered in the name of being "good" or "civilized."

One of my clients experienced this kind of reclamation through her voice. For over twenty years, she successfully facilitated large group strategic sessions in a variety of sectors. Then, in the middle of a high-stakes retreat, her voice suddenly failed her. Air came out of her mouth, but no words formed. The deadly cocktail of stress, sleep deprivation, overcaffeination, and an allergic reaction to the markers she was using triggered a laryngeal spasm.

She finished the session with help from colleagues, but the experience shook her deeply. Every time she stood before a group, she feared her voice might fail again. After a lifetime of success, she found herself incapacitated.

This fear caused her to turn down lucrative work, but the wound ran deeper than money. She described the inability to trust her own voice as "emotionally devastating." It forced her to confront aspects of her shadow: the perfectionism, the control, and the relentless need to look good.

Her healing began in my online Full Voice FUNdamentals course, a five-week journey through the Five Elements Framework. Being playful with her voice and acting silly began to unwind the habitual tension she carried. She became less worried about mistakes or losing control, even in high-pressure situations. Her vocal choices expanded to include more variety of sound. She told me, "These days, I come from the heart more often. If something goes wrong, I can laugh and move on. I'm more willing to be vulnerable, which opens space for others to take risks. The quality of my work with clients has deepened."

Toward the end of the course, she asked how to keep building her vocal strength. I suggested singing. Coincidentally, she lived in a city where one of my friends runs community singing circles, where ordinary people sing just for fun. Now she takes great joy in singing regularly with others. Bringing her voice, flaws and all, into a community of song has deepened her healing and opened a new passion in her life.

So, dear reader, as you inhabit these unfamiliar sounds and characters, I hope you welcome any discomfort with curiosity and kindness. Your shadow is part of what makes you human. It's full of suppressed energy waiting to be of service in your life. Your voice can be a steadfast ally in helping you express your shadow in nourishing, life-giving ways.

Let's end this inquiry with a few questions for reflection:

What parts of yourself have been exiled in the name of being "good"?

What sounds—even in your imagination—might these parts want to make? Try giving one of them thirty seconds of voice. Go ahead. What do you notice?

Your voice is a flashlight. A compass. A release valve.

What's in your basement? Let's find out.

LIMITING VOCAL HABITS

The sound of your voice carries great power. The moment you begin to speak, people are already forming impressions about your credibility, confidence, intelligence, and trustworthiness. You only get a few words to make that first impression.

If the sound of your voice is distracting or grating, your listener may miss the meaning entirely. We've all tuned someone out because their voice didn't land right.

We all have vocal habits. Some enhance communication. Others create subtle (or not so subtle) barriers between our message and the people we're trying to reach.

You might do everything right to prepare—research, organize, practice—only to have your efforts eclipsed by a vocal pattern that undermines your message. That's a high price to pay.

You may already be aware of habits that get in your way, things like:

Mumbling

Speaking too fast

Ending every statement like a question

Sounding too quiet, too monotonous, too young, too tense

Maybe you've cringed at a recording. Maybe someone has given you direct feedback. Even so, knowing a habit isn't the same as knowing how to shift it.

Don't worry. We'll work with all of this as we go.

In the meantime, you might try something brave:

Ask for feedback. Talk to people who know you well and ask what they notice about your voice. Most of us aren't used to listening for vocal patterns, so you may need to guide their attention.

Here are a few questions you can ask:

What qualities do you appreciate about my voice?

Do you think my voice reflects who I am and the gifts I carry?

Are there any vocal habits that interfere with how I communicate?

Has my voice changed over time? If so, what have you noticed?

These conversations can be illuminating and sometimes surprising. You may even inspire others to tune into their own voices as you explore yours.

Limiting vocal habits don't just interfere with communication. They can wear you out. Unless you have an injury or illness, most garden-variety vocal fatigue comes from a lack of full engagement. Here's the usual mix:

Shallow breathing

Tension in the throat or jaw
Disconnection from the body

Add in stress, poor sleep, dehydration, or dry air, and your voice simply can't work the way it was designed to.

Then there's overuse: Three-day trainings. Loud concerts. Sporting events. The kind of full-throttle vocal effort that can leave you raw.

But here's the wild part. You can build vocal strength and endurance, just like a baby.

Yes, really, a baby. Have you ever spent time with a baby in full-blown meltdown? They can cry for hours—red-faced, belly-pumping, fists flailing—and never get hoarse. It's incredible. What's their secret?

Total commitment. That baby isn't multitasking. She's not worrying about dinner plans or college admissions. She's just crying. With every fiber of her being.

That's the kind of embodied energy we'll begin to tap into, not to scream like babies, but to find the clarity and stamina that come from speaking with your whole self.

Many vocal issues can be resolved when your sound is supported by breath, rooted in your body, and aligned with intention.

We'll explore this further as we step into the Five Elements Framework later in this book. Now let's explore how to take care of that voice of yours.

5

CARING FOR YOUR VOICE

We do a lot of things to keep ourselves healthy and safe. We wear seatbelts and bike helmets. We stretch in yoga class. We pick things up using our legs instead of our backs. We build muscle, track steps, and take our vitamins.

But most of us were never taught to care for our voice—this beautiful, intricate, irreplaceable tool we use every day.

Let's change that.

Here are some simple, practical ways to tend your voice with the care it deserves. You'll notice that many of them support your whole well-being because, of course, your voice doesn't live in isolation. It's part of you.

Hydrate, hydrate, hydrate. Your voice works best when it's well watered. Dehydration thickens the mucus that lines your vocal cords and interferes with how they vibrate. Yes, mucus. Sorry. It's not glamorous, but it's real. Aim for your six to eight glasses a day, or more if you're talking a lot, traveling, or in dry air.

Limit caffeine. Caffeine can dry you out. That doesn't mean you need to ditch your beloved coffee or tea; just make sure to **chase each cup with a tall glass of water**. Your voice will thank you.

Get some sleep. Many of us walk through our days in a state of quiet exhaustion. When you're tired, your voice gets gravelly, weak, or hoarse. Sleep matters, not just for cognition and mood, but for vocal recovery. If you snore heavily or deal with sleep apnea, know that these conditions can put serious strain on your voice. If that's part of your experience, consider checking in with a health professional. Your voice deserves rest too.

Move your body. Your voice is not a disembodied instrument: it lives in your whole body. Cardiovascular movement strengthens the breath and muscle support needed for vocal energy and endurance. A moving body means a more alive, supported voice.

Breathe. Let's try something.

Inhale as if you're smelling something wonderful. Exhale with a sigh of pleasure. Simple, right? This kind of breathing brings you into the parasympathetic nervous system—your rest-and-digest state—and also fuels your voice.

There are lots of wonderful breathing exercises online (including some of mine!). Explore, play, and practice bringing breath back into conscious relationship with sound.

Soften the tension. Your neck. Your jaw. Your throat. Your face. Tension here can clamp down your voice and your presence.

Try a big, fake yawn (with sound).

Massage your jaw. Roll your neck slowly like seaweed in a gentle tide. Your voice will open. And those around you might soften in response too.

Address your allergies. Seasonal allergies often overload the system with mucus, leading to nasal tone, muffled speech, throat irritation, and postnasal drip. Frequent throat clearing and coughing can inflame the vocal cords. Treating your allergies gently and early is a gift to your voice, and to your listeners.

Skip the shouting. Repeated bouts of yelling can cause vocal nodes: calluses on the vocal cords that interfere with vibration. Yes, you can make loud sounds without damaging your voice, but that requires serious technique and intentional breath support. Unless you're trained in vocal athletics (or you're a crying baby, as I previously discussed), it's best to avoid unconscious screaming for long periods of time.

When in doubt, get checked out. Chronic hoarseness, soreness, or coughing are not just part of talking. They may be signs of acid reflux, infection, inflammation, or other issues that need medical attention.

Please don't ignore them. And please don't push through them with the exercises in this book until you've gotten clear about what's going on. Your voice deserves the same care you'd give to any other part of your body.

Humidify your space. Especially in winter or arid climates, dry air can parch the vocal cords. A bedroom humidifier or a steamy shower can be incredibly helpful.

Warm up gently. Just as you wouldn't sprint without warming up your legs, your voice benefits from gentle, playful warm-ups. Even humming can help. (More on this later.)

Your voice has worked hard for you, often without thanks or rest. Let this be a new way of being in relationship with it. Not just as a tool, but as a cherished companion.

Before we move into the expressive practices of the Five Elements Framework, let's take a moment to tune inward. This breath ritual is a way to come home to your body, your breath, and the voice that lives within both.

You don't need to sit a certain way. Just find a posture that feels both alert and relaxed (whatever that means for you right now).

Let your eyes close, if that feels safe, or simply soften your gaze.

Inhale gently through your nose as though you are smelling something you love: fresh basil, warm cookies, a pine forest after rain.

Exhale with a soft sigh, letting your belly relax and shoulders drop. Let the sound be unfiltered, just as it wants to come.

Repeat this series several times, savoring the sensations.

Next, bring a hand to your lower belly. Feel its rise and fall. Let the breath move in and out without control.

Gently begin to add a little sound to your exhale. It doesn't need to be beautiful or correct. Maybe it's a low hum. Maybe it's an "ahhh." Maybe it's something completely your own. Let the sound ride the breath like sea-foam on a wave: effortless, easy, connected.

Try another one of these, listening for the sound that wants to ride out on your breath.

Listen to the resonance that lingers: the presence of voice even in silence.

This is your starting place.

Not performance. Not perfection.

Just being here—with yourself, your breath, your sound.

6

MY VOCAL STORY

Earlier I invited you to explore your own vocal story. Now it's time to share mine. It's foundational to how I created this work.

I was a shy, quirky, and anxious kid—way too tall and way too smart. I grew up singing in good choirs and doing some theater, but I never sang alone in front of anyone.

Not friends. Not family. Nobody. The thought of it terrified me.

That fear is common, of course, but in my family, solo singers were all around me. Why couldn't I do what they did?

In my early twenties, through a series of strange events, I found myself singing solo with my friend's jazz trio at a historic hotel on the Mississippi River. That first summer, I was nearly paralyzed by stage fright. Frustrated and shaky, I hired a therapist and a voice coach to help me sort it out.

The therapist helped me unravel the roots of my fear: family dynamics, cultural stories, and a tangle of internalized expectations.

The voice coach had another idea. She suggested I take a workshop with members of the Roy Hart Centre, a teaching community in southern France devoted to full-range vocal expression.

The idea filled me with dread. But somehow, someone in my mouth said yes. And off I went to a church basement in Minneapolis.

When I walked into that workshop, I had a strong story about who I was and what my voice could do: I was shy. I was neurotic. I was a hot mess. My voice was low, with a range that stopped cold when it got to a certain note. Beyond that note was nothing. Just silence.

During the workshop, one of the teachers, Saule Ryan, took me on a vocal adventure that led me almost to the top of the piano. I was stunned. I thought my voice ended after that one note, and I had just made sound *all the way up there*?

What made that possible? A few crucial things.

First and foremost was Saule's kind and persistent encouragement. Also, the fact that the sounds didn't need to be pretty or correct. Most importantly, I wasn't myself while I made them.

I was pretending to be a huge hawk.

That fierce, untamed energy cracked something open in me. Sounds came out of my mouth that I'd never imagined were mine. And I loved it.

I realized that no one had ever asked me for *all* the voice I had. And like most of us, I had a lot.

All my life, I'd been encouraged to quiet down, be nice, and blend in. This experience of full expression rewrote my story.

It shattered the limits I thought were fixed.

It made me question the shape I thought was me.

I remember asking myself:

"What else am I wrong about?"

"How else is my story too small?"

That's what led me deeper: to study with Roy Hart teachers in Minneapolis, Toronto, and their center in France.

As I explored, I started noticing how certain sounds seemed to originate in different parts of the body. That led me to the chakra system in the yogic tradition. I also became fascinated by Jung's work on archetypes, shadow, and the collective unconscious, and how those forces are expressed through the voice.

At the same time, in my work as an organizational development consultant, I was observing leaders in action. Because I was steeped in vocal exploration, I started seeing patterns. I noticed how leaders' voices affected their presence, relationships, and effectiveness. I saw how much a voice could reveal and how changing the voice could change a life.

Over time those observations coalesced into the Five Elements Framework. I began using it to coach people struggling with their voices, including leaders referred by my organizational colleagues.

In the decades since, I've shared this work with leaders from every sector as well as attorneys, engineers, clergy, therapists, coaches, educators, performers, salespeople, and health professionals.

In 2011, I wrote my first book: *Full Voice: The Art and Practice of Vocal Presence.* Now I'm training others to carry the work forward in places I had never imagined at first. There are now twenty Full Voice coaches and fifty full voice trainers in North America, Europe, and Australia, and more are being trained all the time.

My vocal liberation spilled into songwriting. I've written dozens of songs and recorded nine albums of original music. And I've become a leader in the flourishing global community singing movement, an ever-growing field, rooted in the conviction that everyone deserves to sing, regardless of training or ability.

As I look back on this long and winding vocal journey, one thing becomes clear:

My own voice was the engine that carried me through it all.

If anything I've shared here stirred insights in you, feel free to pause and write some reflections of your own. Let your voice speak to you—in memory, in image, and in sound.

{PART TWO}

The Five Elements Framework

7

OVERVIEW

Sound, when stretched, is music.
Movement, when stretched, is dance.
Mind, when stretched, is meditation.
Life, when stretched, is celebration.

—RAVI SHANKAR

The Five Elements Framework is a proven, practical, and playful way to stretch your sound, your listening, your leadership, and your life. It offers a map to expand your vocal awareness and flexibility so you can communicate more powerfully, clearly, and authentically with the people around you.

In this section, we'll explore the five elements: Earth, Fire, Water, Metal, and Air. For every element, you'll learn:

- Where it's sourced in the body
- How to access it through playful sound exercises
- What qualities it can evoke in your leadership and relationships

The goal here is not performance. It's reclamation.

As you build vocal range and awareness, you'll be able to shift your voice with intention. When you need to convey gravitas, your voice will be strong and grounded. When you want to spark enthusiasm, your fiery voice will ignite the room. When someone is hurting, your voice will wrap them in care.

You'll move beyond habitual vocal patterns into a fuller, freer expression of who you truly are.

Here is what makes this framework distinct:

1. We focus on sound, beyond mere speaking and singing. Most people rarely explore the full range of their voice. Sure, you might stretch out when you yawn or shout when you stub your toe or playfully coo at a child. But in everyday life, we tend to stay in a narrow band of expression, especially when we're being "professional."

Logical sentences have their place, but they only use a fraction of the sounds available to you. The Five Elements Framework helps you recover a wilder, wider vocal range, one that also reconnects you to the parts of your humanity that may have been tucked away over time.

2. We use *archetypes* and *characters* to exaggerate the sound of each element, often in ways that are silly, dramatic, even ridiculous.

Why? Because it works.

Characters like a swaggering Italian tenor, a giant stomping through the forest, or a delicate British dame can help you slip past your usual vocal identity. They act like booster rockets, helping you escape the gravitational pull of habit.

Sometimes it's easier to make a big change than a small one. Once you find the exaggerated version, you can dial it back into something usable in everyday conversation. Later, when you need to recall a sound, these archetypes become anchors: "What was that Fire voice again? Ah, yes—the Italian tenor!"

When you engage your body, emotions, imagination, and a little risk, your learning goes deeper and lasts longer.

3. This work invites you to *play*. Leaders rarely get the opportunity to cut loose and get wild. Many of my clients tell me they feel more alive, more human, after doing this work. Once they move past the awkwardness, they treasure the chance to be loud, strange, tender, and even absurd.

So go ahead. Dare to look silly. As my mentor, leadership author Peter Block, likes to say: "The only thing you have to lose is the respect of your peers!"

As we begin, you'll likely discover that some elements feel like home, while others might feel foreign or uncomfortable. That's normal. We tend to avoid what we're not good at, but growth lives at the edge of discomfort.

So stay curious.

If you feel resistant to something, ask yourself: "Is this resistance physical? Emotional? Whose voice am I hearing in my head right now?"

If something feels delightful, ask: "Where do I feel this in my body? What memory or freedom is this sound unlocking?"

Each of the five elements has unique gifts:

Earth grounds you, connects you to gut instinct, and conveys authority.

Fire awakens vitality, fuels passion, and helps you to be seen and heard.

Water expresses the heart: care, empathy, and emotional depth.

Metal sharpens clarity and volume without strain.

Air brings possibility, imagination, and spiritual connection.

By the end of this book, I hope you'll know how to access them in your own voice and use them with intention.

Let's begin our exploration together.

SAMPLING THE FIVE ELEMENTS FRAMEWORK

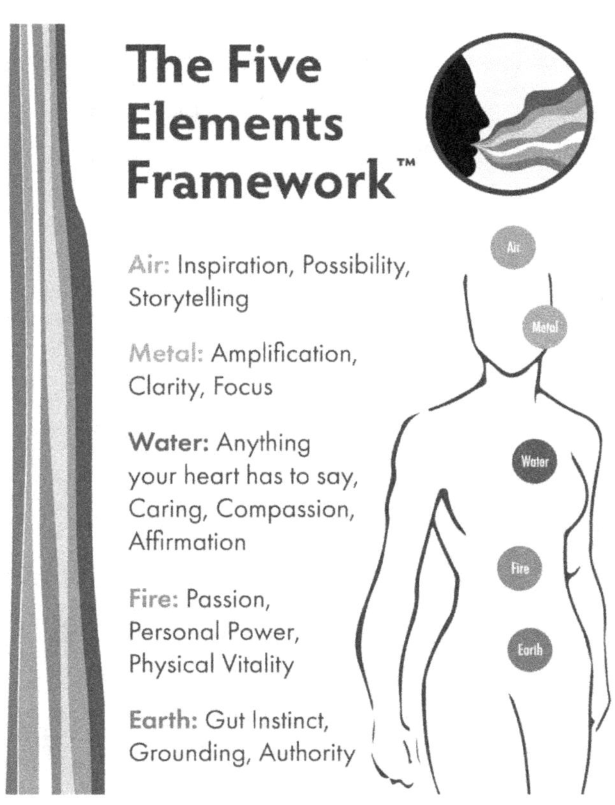

It's time to sample the five elements using your own voice. Just a taste. Just enough to get a sense of each one.

You may not be in a place where you can make unusual sounds right now. Maybe you're in an office with thin walls or on a treadmill at the gym, or your kids are sleeping just down the hall.

Please do what you can in your current context. If you can't make much noise right now, just keep reading. You can always try the sounds later in the car, the shower, or some other sound-friendly place.

For this quick preview, we'll do three things for each element:

1. Identify where the element is sourced in the body
2. Explore a playful sound using a character
3. Discover what the sound is good for in leadership and life

In the next chapters, we'll go much deeper into each element.

The Earth Voice

The **Earth** voice is sourced in your feet, legs, hips, and pelvis.

The character we'll use to sample it is a sleepy caveman.

Try making a few deep, relaxed yawning sounds. If this exercise inspires you to yawn, please do so.

Feel free to add some sound and a nice stretch while you're at it!

Earth in everyday speech is great for:

- Projecting authority
- Getting grounded
- Accessing your gut instinct

The Fire Voice

The Fire voice is sourced in the belly and solar plexus.

The character we'll use to sample Fire is a martial artist.

Stand up if you are able. Plant your feet solidly on the ground. Then punch with a fully extended arm while shouting, "Kee-ya!"

Repeat this a few more times, feeling the physical energy driving your sound.

Fire in everyday speech is great for:

- Expressing passion
- Being seen and heard
- Waking up physical vitality

The Water Voice

Water is sourced in the heart and throat area.

The character we'll use to sample it is a sad dog. Picture a bloodhound with the droopy face and give a few long, mournful howls.

Repeat this a few more times, imagining your pack howling along.

Water in everyday speech is perfect for:

- Sharing care and compassion
- Offering affirmation or apology
- Speaking with warmth from the heart

The Metal Voice

The Metal voice is sourced in the eyes and forehead.

We'll use a whining child to get a taste of the sound.

Try saying "Mom!" with your brattiest voice. Really lean into the whine until you feel it in your nose.

Try a few more with increasing brattiness.

Metal in everyday speech is good for:

- Getting loud without strain
- Sharpening clarity
- Focusing attention

The Air Voice

The last of the five, the Air voice, is sourced in the crown of the head.

I'll invite you to make a few sounds as a delighted baby to try this one out.

Take a big breath. Open your eyes and mouth with a great sigh of delight, "Aaaaaah!"

Repeat this a few times, feeling the air moving through your mouth.

Air is ideal for:

- Storytelling
- Expressing ideas and possibilities
- Kindling spiritual connection

There you have it: a quick, playful introduction to the Five Elements Framework.

Take a moment now.

How are you feeling compared to when you began?

Did certain sounds feel familiar?

Were some difficult or unreachable?

Did any surprise you or rub you the wrong way?

Feel free to reflect or take notes.

Sometimes even these brief experiments can stir up more than we expect.

Now that you've had a taste, you've got what I like to call the "secret decoder ring for voices."

In the coming chapters, we'll explore each element in depth, including how leaders use these voices in their every-day work.

But before we dive deeper, I want to share one more story: a glimpse into the origins of this extended-range vocal work, where it came from, and why it matters.

9

ORIGIN STORY

This story begins in Germany over a century ago, in the brutal trench warfare of World War I.

An eighteen-year-old German Jew named Alfred Wolfsohn is serving as a stretcher-bearer on the Western Front. Day after day, he witnesses horrors beyond imagination and hears the cries of wounded soldiers echo in his psyche.

After the war Wolfsohn is left shattered. He suffers from what we now call PTSD, including relentless auditory hallucinations of those anguished cries. His mind plays them on a loop over and over again.

Out of desperation to find peace, he begins to make the sounds himself. He mimics the cries. The screams. The moans. And slowly something shifts.

Through this strange and courageous vocal catharsis, Wolfsohn begins to heal. He eventually recovers his mental and spiritual health and with it, a conviction that voice holds power far beyond conventional ideas of speech or song.

Wolfsohn escapes Hitler's Germany and finds refuge in London. There he begins experimenting with extended-range vocalizing as a tool for healing, self-discovery, and transformation, first on his own and then with others.

As Wolfsohn's health declines, one of his protégés—a gifted Jewish South African actor named Roy Hart—carries the work forward. Hart expands the practice into avant-garde theater. He forms a performing company that pushes the boundaries of vocal expression. The company eventually moves from London to a ramshackle chateau in the south of France.

Shortly after the move, tragedy strikes: Hart and two other company members are killed in a car accident during a tour in Spain.

But the work doesn't die with them. Several members of the company step forward, choosing to continue, evolve, and pass on what they've learned. One of those people is my beloved teacher, friend, and colleague Saule Ryan. He sets me on the path to vocal freedom in that church basement in Minneapolis in the late 1980s.

Saule connects me to other Roy Hart teachers in France and Canada, who guide my continued learning. Over time Saule and I begin coleading vocal workshops together in the United States, a collaboration that endures for over twenty years until he turns eighty and retires from travel.

To this day every person I train in this work learns how to share this origin story. At the end of their training, I introduce them to Saule over Zoom so they can connect to the living thread of this legacy.

It is one of the greatest privileges of my life to be part of this lineage. I hope with all my heart that I honor it through the work I do.

In the next chapter, we'll explore the Earth voice in more depth: grounding down into the body, the breath, and the roots of presence.

THE EARTH VOICE: ROCK-SOLID

As we enter each of the five elements in more depth, you'll be invited to make more sustained sound across a broader range using audio tracks on my website. Here are a few guidelines to support that journey:

Take exquisite care of yourself. Notice when you're nearing your limits and choose consciously how far to go. If something hurts, stop.

At the same time, be brave. Take risks. Play.

Welcome emotion. Voice can open surprising doors to feeling.

Stay curious—bring a spirit of gentleness and wonder.

Make whatever sounds you can in your current context. Don't wake the baby or alarm the neighbors.

Now let's dig into the Earth voice.

To awaken what you already know about this voice, let's begin with some images:

- A mama bear rumbling low to protect her cubs
- Darth Vader saying, "Luke, I am your father"

- Bea Arthur as Dorothy on *The Golden Girls* drawling sarcasm through clenched teeth
- A department store Santa booming, "Ho, ho, ho!"
- Johnny Cash growling, "I fell into a burning ring of fire"
- A chain-smoking blues singer dragging emotion through every syllable
- Eeyore from *Winnie the Pooh* intoning his depressive "Don't mind me . . ."
- A cello ringing through a stone church

Some famous Earth voices include Leonard Cohen, Whoopi Goldberg, Morgan Freeman, Tracy Chapman, Scarlett Johansson, Viola Davis, Arnold Schwarzenegger, Jane Fonda, and Nick Cave. Can you think of others?

The Earth voice is sourced in the feet, legs, hips, and pelvic bowl. You won't necessarily feel vibrations there, but accessing Earth sound requires a connection to your lower body. This voice helps you ground your presence, tune into gut instinct, and embody natural authority.

Begin opening up the Earth voice by faking or making a yawn with a little sound, as we did in chapter 8. You'll probably keep yawning after this first one, so go ahead and take a few more. Can you feel the sweet stretch in your jaw and throat? Are your shoulders and neck relaxing? Do you enjoy the rush of oxygen to your brain? Are you sensing a vibration in your chest? Enjoy all of that.

Voicing your yawn is one of the quickest ways to access the Earth sound. (But maybe avoid doing it in the middle of a high-stakes meeting!) I'll offer other Earth vocal exercises later in this chapter and in the online resources at my website.

This grounded gravitas is one that we leaders must cultivate, especially in chaotic or uncertain times. When I encounter a client with a rock-solid Earth voice, I ask them, "Tell me: are you the person in the room who stays calm in an emergency when everyone around you is panicking?" They pause, reflect, and with a proud little smile say, "Yes. That's me." The voice gives me a clue; the question gives me confirmation.

Sometimes that same client has come to me to enliven his voice beyond a dull monotone. What can be an asset in one setting—grounding calm—can become a liability in another: a droning monotone. It's all about being familiar with your vocal options.

Let me share a story about one of my clients, an Ivy League professor and entrepreneur who has a deep, steady Earth voice. This vocal quality served him well in his hypnosis work with clients experiencing debilitating anxiety. Now as a leader of his own training company, his voice helps convey calm, authority, and trust.

But the Earth voice can also lull. When he gave talks to larger audiences, he unintentionally hypnotized them to the point of losing their attention. He's not the only client whose Earth voice put people to sleep. The same quality that soothes in one setting can sedate in another.

We worked together to bring more Fire into his delivery, not by replacing Earth but by expanding his expressive range. The sounds came easily, but culturally they were unfamiliar. As a tall, strong Midwestern man, he'd spent his life dialing himself down. He didn't want to intimidate. But with practice he learned to wield a Fire voice when needed while keeping his grounded Earth voice close at hand.

The Earth voice is also good for connecting to your gut instinct. Your gut (or second brain) contains 100 million neurons and a complicated network of neurotransmitters and proteins that are attuned to stress and pleasure, much like the brain in your skull. It has its own intelligence, but you have to learn to tune into it.

In the headlong rush of the workplace, the slow, deep nudging that comes from the gut can be hard to hear. We live in a world that always inviting us to speed up. Our computers are lightning fast. We're buzzed on caffeine. We breathlessly dash from meeting to meeting. We're running behind. We're trying to catch up. Our language reveals this manic pace.

For a leader, it takes commitment and practice to slow down enough to access gut wisdom. This indispensable intelligence can help you make the right hires, ask smarter questions, tune into tensions before they explode, and choose the most fruitful strategies. Sinking into the Earth voice regularly supports you in cultivating (and trusting) this ancient way of knowing.

This vocal tone is also a useful choice for projecting authority, for accessing your alpha power. Even in the most civilized settings, we are all carrying our animal natures with us. The amygdala, part of our mammalian brain, is constantly scanning for danger, processing emotions, and checking on the pecking order. We've all known leaders who operate solely from the reptile brain, and we've witnessed the damage it can do when it's running the show.

I'm not suggesting that you become one of them. I do want you to know how to give voice to your natural authority.

Another client, a retired public sector leader, discovered her voice of authority in a surprising way. We worked together on Zoom during the pandemic, ostensibly to improve her singing voice. She was one of the many people who took up ukulele during this time and wanted to sing along with more ease and pleasure. But before we could work on that, we had to deal with her puppy.

He kept interrupting our sessions. I noticed that when she corrected him, the voice she used to was soft, high, and ineffective. She'd coo, "Down, Bailey! No, Bailey!"

I told her, "You need to learn how to talk to him like the alpha dog."

The Earth voice *is* the voice of the alpha.

She tried it, and it worked like magic. The dog started listening, and his behavior eventually improved. She reflected how helpful accessing her Earth voice would have been during her career, especially when her leadership was questioned.

We were finally able to get to work on her singing.

Now I'm not recommending that you speak to the board of directors the way you would to a misbehaving puppy. But I do encourage you to remember that the reptile brain is still shaping our behavior more than we care to admit.

There are times when you as a leader need to be the alpha in the room. To say a solid no when necessary. To interrupt an injustice. To claim your right to speak uninterrupted. To affirm that you know what you're doing. To be rooted like a great tree as the fierce winds of change blow all around you.

Before I invite you to open up your Earth voice, let's talk about the Five Elements practices: what they are like, why they work, and how to make the best use of them.

The Five Elements practices are, well, quite strange. I designed them that way on purpose. The fact that they are so bizarre, so outside of your regular way of expressing yourself, will help you remember the experience later. These practices engage you physically and emotionally as well as inviting a measure of risk. Eventually you'll be able to access a more subtle version of the sound naturally, but for now, we're stretching the boundaries of sound, identity, gender, and even species in a spirit of play and exploration.

As you explore these practices, it's key to pay attention.

What physical sensations are you noticing?

Any internal dialogue running through your mind?

How about memories or images arising?

Most of us have the habit of jumping to conclusions about an experience right away, especially one that is uncomfortable. We move too swiftly to our intellect and miss out on the other capacities we carry as embodied humans: wonder, emotions, surprise, and curiosity. I invite you to linger in your full range of responses for as long as you can without crafting a story to contain them. Marinate in whatever arises from these practices, and your voice will have a chance to offer its undiscovered gifts to you.

It's also important to notice when you're hitting a vocal, physical, or emotional limit.

If something hurts, stop.

If you start coughing, stop.

You are in charge of your yeses and nos in this process.

Continue to hydrate during and after these practices. They are another kind of physical workout, and you're detoxing some cultural and emotional stuff you'd do best to wash away.

Welcome your nervousness and self-consciousness as part of the process. Be kind to the part of you that's afraid—and then keep going.

Notice the stories that arise, but don't let them shut you down.

Finally, remember to invite joy and pleasure into these practices. You can learn a lot while feeling delicious.

Now we'll dive into a few practices for connecting to your Earth voice. There's no one right way to access this sound. In nature, Earth expresses itself in a wide variety of ways: boulders, sand, mud, pebbles, and mountains. Why would it be any different with your voice?

As a way to prepare for these practices, I suggest getting down on the ground if you are able. This sound is all about gravity. Lie on your back and feel the muscles relax against the floor. Soften your jaw and neck. Breathe into your belly. You may want to try a very slow roll to one side, keeping everything soft and floppy as you do. And making some low, soft sounds will help you surrender your weight.

The first character we'll use to deepen into Earth is the giant. Imagine being eight feet tall with huge feet and a bad temper. Your hairy chest swells with indignation. Your brow furrows. If your body and circumstances allow, stand up and stomp around as you say, "Fee fi fo fum!"

Please go to www.barbaramcafee.com/full-voice-for-leaders to access guided Earth voice exercises using several different characters. You'll also hear one of my songs, "Taste of Midnight," which exemplifies the Earth voice in song.

After exploring these sounds, feel free to reflect on these questions:

What did you discover about your own Earth voice?

Was the sound familiar, foreign, or somewhere in between?

How did it feel in your body?

Are there places in your life and leadership where you need more rootedness?

Do you know people who embody this voice?

What qualities in them do you admire?

Feel free to pause and make a few notes.

I'll close the Earth voice chapter by sharing a deeper teaching that this voice offers about how we strive.

When you approach your lowest vocal register, you're meeting a limit. You can't push to get there. You have to soften, deepen, and open into the sound.

Earth teaches us that not all power comes from tension or force.

For me as a leader, this question has become a touchstone: "What becomes possible when I strive by going down and in rather than up and out?"

Now it's time to shift up and out into the Fire voice.

11

THE FIRE VOICE: HERE I AM, WORLD!

You've probably heard the expression "fire in the belly." That's exactly where this vocal power lives: in your belly and solar plexus. When you speak with Fire, you don't just make sound, you ignite presence. It literally heats up your body with vital energy.

Here are some examples of Fire voices that you are likely to recognize:

Sports fans hollering with joy as their team wins the championship.

Martin Luther King Jr. delivers his "I Have a Dream" speech at the 1963 Civil Rights March on Washington.

Oprah Winfrey shouts from the TV stage: "You get a car and you get a car and you get a car! Everybody gets a car!"

An operatic tenor brings down the house with a powerful aria.

Dr. Brené Brown speaks powerfully about vulnerability from the TEDx stage.

Greta Thunberg confronts the United Nations Climate Summit with a fierce, tearful "How dare you!"

An irritable New York City cabdriver yells out the window during a traffic jam.

Some other famous examples of the Fire voice include: Tina Turner, Mick Jagger, Cher, Bruce Springsteen, Bonnie Raitt, Freddie Mercury, and Cynthia Erivo, as well as flamenco and mariachi singers.

Can you think of others?

The Fire voice is useful for expressing passion, being seen and heard, and activating physical vitality.

I'll invite you to start opening up the Fire sound by shouting "Hey!" several times. Imagine you are trying to get someone's attention in a crowd. Can you feel the heat of this sound starting to build? We'll stoke this fire higher with more practices later in this chapter.

Like all of these elements, Fire is great until it isn't. Let me share a client story about how one man discovered how to use his Fire well. Many years ago, an educational consultant and author engaged me as a voice coach to help him become more effective at presenting his work with purpose, meaning, and resonance.

As a former classroom teacher, he had cultivated a powerful Fire voice. This is a common voice for many educators, as they are required to project their voices in classrooms, usually without amplification. It also reflected his passion for his topic, which is one of the primary uses of the Fire voice. However, his unrelenting Fire could become overbearing and mask the more tender aspects of his message. This was especially true when he used a microphone. His amplified Fire voice tended to be harsh and strident.

In our work together, he discovered how to bring more variety into his presentations, matching the vocal tone to the particular message he was delivering. He was surprised to find that bringing more nuance and softness into his voice opened up some vulnerability that his habitual Fire voice had masked. Unmodulated Fire can start to scorch. Without the balance of pause, empathy, or curiosity, a fiery delivery can overwhelm the listener or flatten nuance. Once he grew accustomed to bringing more heart to his speaking, he saw the positive impact on the educators he was addressing.

Much of this man's work focuses on helping educators in international schools to communicate more effectively. Over the past fifteen years, he has incorporated the Five Elements Framework into his presentations to illustrate the impact of an instructor's voice on how pupils learn. His audiences include people from every corner of the world. Throughout the time he has been presenting the Five Elements to thousands of people, its validity has held up across these diverse cultures. I'm touched that he has carried this work so far into the world and brought back valuable insights about its efficacy with such a wide variety of people.

Fire is also a good choice for public speaking—for being seen and heard. Public speaking can be excruciating for many people, especially if they tend toward introversion. Many of my voice clients are introverted leaders who know they need to expand their vocal communication skills and want to do so in a way that feels authentic.

For introverts, full expression is a bit like a second language. It won't flow as easily as it does for extraverts. On the other hand, many people live very well using a second or even third language. The introvert will never be the loudest person in the room, full of noise and bravado, nor should they be. Introverted leaders bring many invaluable gifts to their organizations: deep listening, empathy, calm, and thoughtful decision-making. They can find ways to use their voices well with two more introvert superpowers: preparation and practice.

Here is the story of how one introverted leader found his authentic public speaking voice. The president of a large architectural firm engaged me after seeing himself on a corporate promotional video. In it he spoke words of great passion and commitment to the organization's work but did so in a tone that was flat and dull. His facial expression was also at complete odds with his words. He was both surprised and horrified at the gap between his internal conviction and his external delivery. He was on a quest to discover how to bring his passion out in a way that felt authentic to him.

We began his work by taking him through all Five Elements in an exaggerated way. When he opened up his Fire voice, we were both surprised. Out of this typically soft-spoken man came a big, resonant, fiery sound! The Fire voice reminded him of the bold, brassy sound of the trombone he played as a teenager. He wondered if he chose his instrument back then as a way to safely express his Fire energy. I sent him home with several rock and roll songs to get him accustomed to the way Fire felt in his voice, body, and psyche. He loved these songs, and they became part of his daily commute.

Our work then turned to reconnecting his voice to his physical vitality, which is another gift of Fire. This project involved some vigorous and often hilarious exercises. To get his lower body activated, we stood back-to-back with our knees bent and attempted to push each other across the room while he made long, strong sounds. He pretended to throw his sound like a baseball. He practiced the opening of a coming presentation in the character of a fiery preacher, striding around and waving his arms. The next step invited him to keep this physical and vocal engagement while he stood still.

His diligent practice paid off. He found a way to incorporate more energy into his everyday speech with his colleagues while still feeling like himself. When he was invited to present at a prestigious international conference, his vibrant and engaging presence resulted in many new connections.

This man is still an introvert by nature. He still speaks calmly and thinks deeply. But when he needs to bring some Fire, he can tap into his inner trombone with ease.

When introverts prepare and practice, their voices can burn steady and bright, like coals rather than fireworks.

As I just mentioned, the Fire voice charges up your body with energy and vitality. That kind of aliveness is a necessary asset for a leader. It provides the energy you need to face challenges with courage. In many cultures around the world, people perform vigorous dances and chants in their preparations for battle. One example is the *haka*, a ceremonial chant and movement practice from the Māori people of New Zealand. While it is widely known as a preparation for battle, the haka is also a ritual of unity, storytelling, and strength. Seeing the haka helps me understand how disembodied and rigid dominant Western norms have become by contrast.

Physical vitality also creates the stamina required to hold complexity, conflict, grief, and uncertainty without burning out.

Now let's stoke our Fire voices with a few practices.

Before we do, here's a suggestion: if you find yourself getting hoarse or tight from making the strong Fire sounds, try incorporating more physical energy into the practice. Remember what you discovered from that crying baby?

You'll also need to find a place to make a lot of noise. Fire can get loud. I'm astonished at how few places there are that allow us to get as loud as we can be. Some possible locales for making big noise include the shower, car, beach, garage, or (if they are of the correct age and disposition) with children.

You may also notice tension when you start to get loud, especially if you aren't loud and forceful by nature. The habit of self-censorship can cause muscle tension that inhibits the full expression of the sound. You may hear echoes of voices from your past trying to shut you down. This is a common experience. After making strong Fire sounds, many of my clients wonder aloud if the police are going to show up. Bring patience and curiosity to all that arises.

Let's do a little warmup to get your body and voice ready for fire.

Stand up.

Stride around.

Swing your arms.

Beat your chest like Tarzan.

Take a power stance, standing tall and spreading your arms and legs wide.

Take up as much space as you possibly can.

Please go to www.barbaramcafee.com/full-voice-for-leaders to access guided Fire voice exercises using several different characters. You'll also hear one of my songs, "Heart of a Warrior," which exemplifies the Fire voice in song.

After exploring these sounds, reflect on these questions:

What did you discover about your own Fire voice?

Was the sound familiar, foreign, or somewhere in between?

How did it feel in your body?

Where in your life are you longing to be more visible, more passionate, more alive?

What's holding back the spark? What might shift if you let that Fire speak?

Do you know people who embody this voice? What qualities in them do you admire?

One of the deeper lessons of the Fire voice is accessing power without tension. Much of our leadership language includes words like *drive*, *push*, *strive*, and *grit*. That type of strength is required at times, but I wonder how often we are overworking. I know that for much of my life, I've carried the habit of trying too hard. The Fire voice can provide some intriguing reflections on that pattern.

It's common to bring a great deal of tension into making the Fire sound at first. The neck muscles tighten. The brow furrows into a stormy frown. Fists clench. This tension hinders the sound. Unless you have a vocal injury, it's possible to make a powerful, full-throated Fire sound while relaxed. You can experiment with this by standing (if you are able) and speaking loudly while gently rolling your neck and shoulders. Can you keep the sound going if you relax your jaw and face? How about if you slowly circle your hips as well?

This inquiry has shifted my assumptions about my own leadership. Other leaders have found it fruitful as well. It opens questions like:

What does it mean to be strong and relaxed at the same time?

How do I hinder true power through the habits of tension and trying?

What does this experiment reveal about my relationship with my own power?

Do other questions arise for you?

Now that we've kindled the Fire voice, let's dive into the next sound: Water.

12

THE WATER VOICE: FINDING THE FLOW

The Water voice lives in the tender terrain of the heart and throat.

Here are some examples of Water voices that you are likely to recognize:

A weary parent murmurs a lullaby to a fretful baby at 3 a.m.

Former U.S. president Jimmy Carter delivers a moving speech about his work with Habitat for Humanity.

An operatic alto moves her audience to tears through her rendition of a tragic aria by Verdi.

A mediator invites a divorcing couple to pause and find calm before resuming negotiations.

Robin Williams embodies an elderly British nanny in the 1993 film *Mrs. Doubtfire.*

A hospice chaplain brings words of comfort to a patient in their final days of life.

Other famous examples of the Water voice include crooners like Tony Bennett and Nat King Cole, Billie Holiday,

Fred Rogers, Norah Jones, Bon Iver, Judy Garland, and Leslie Odom Jr. I have also noticed that many songs about water, like "Moon River" and "Shenandoah," sound best when sung with the Water voice.

Can you think of others?

This element is for expressing anything your heart has to say: things like compassion, caring, welcome, affirmation, or apology.

Let's briefly sample the Water sound together. We'll explore more practices for opening up Water later in this chapter. Go ahead and try a few enthusiastic "woo's," as though you're cheering on your favorite band or sports team.

The Water voice is warm and inviting. When people hear it, they feel safe, seen, and welcome. Many people in the helping professions, such as therapists, social workers, and chaplains use this voice. Their conversations with people are generally one-on-one or in small groups and can often touch on tender subjects.

Many times leaders need to function as healers. Here are a few circumstances when your Water voice is an ideal choice:

- Offering comfort during a time of grief, loss, or failure
- Naming collective pain during organizational upheavals or societal traumas
- Repairing a breach of trust after a mistake
- Navigating uncertainty or ambiguity, when answers just aren't clear
- Deescalating conflict
- Marking a threshold such as a retirement or the completion of a long journey together
- Catching burnout before collapse

The Water voice helps us to honor the humanity of the people around us and our own as well. One of my clients experienced a layoff after fifteen years of devoting long hours and untiring commitment to his company. He told me that his boss's delivery of the news, brusquely and without eye contact, made the experience much more traumatic than it needed to be. I know many leaders who have been doing the layoffs. They are in need of healing Water as well.

Like with all of the voices, there are circumstances when the Water voice doesn't work at all. Many people who express themselves primarily in Water have the experience of total strangers confiding in them. "I've never told anyone this before, but I'm going to tell you now . . ." There may be times when they aren't interested in hearing everyone's most cherished secrets. Sometimes people with Water voices also have a difficult time with conflict or setting clear boundaries. This voice is also a poor choice for public speaking. Your listeners may enjoy a nice little snooze and entirely miss your message.

Here is a beautiful tale about a client who rediscovered her Water voice and all that unfolded when she did. Early in her career in the film business, my client adopted the habit of speaking loud and fast in order to make herself heard. She was a diminutive Asian woman in rooms full of older white men, who often overlooked or interrupted her. To build her credibility, she altered her voice and mannerisms to be more traditionally masculine. She learned to speak forcefully and quickly in a tone lower than her natural voice.

When she moved to a different company with a more diverse workforce, she assumed that her new coworkers didn't like her or her ideas. It seemed as though every time she offered something, it was rejected. Confused and disheartened, she sought vocal coaching from me to become a more effective communicator in her new position.

I soon discovered that this woman was all Fire all the time. Even though her circumstances had changed, the old habits were still at play. After opening up all five elements, we focused our work on bringing more of the Water sound into her speaking voice.

First, we explored how to recognize the way the Water sound felt in her body. I had her stand and sway while making soothing sounds. Then we sought out a character that would help her give voice to Water. She immediately knew whom to choose as her ally: a woman she knew well who exemplified the kind of warm, engaging tone my client wanted to emulate. Thinking about this friend became a mnemonic device for accessing that vocal quality. Finally, we found a few simple songs—lullabies and love songs—that helped her practice the flowing sound in flowing songs.

After these initial sessions, she took some time to practice and experiment on her own. When we reconvened a few weeks later, she reported some seismic shifts at work. It turns out that people liked her just fine and really loved her ideas. The resistance she had sensed had little to do with her or her content and was focused instead on the intensity of her communication style. Her relationships with her teammates became more collaborative and relaxed. The ideas she brought to the table were welcomed and appreciated. Not only did the Water voice affect her relationships with her colleagues, it also shifted her well-being. She let go of the habit of pushing and the intensity that can come with constant Fire. Her nervous system settled down. She lightened up.

With all of that success at work, she decided to experiment with bringing more Water into how she communicated with her family at home. She described her husband as "a pretty watery guy": easy-going, warm, and tender-hearted. He was a willing participant in the exploration. As she brought more gentleness and flow into their household, they both noticed a significant and delicious shift. The atmosphere in their household became more peaceful. They opened up fresh conversations about their relationship—what it had been and what they were wanting to build. Letting go of so much habitual Fire energy allowed my client to thrive at new levels both at work and at home.

Her ability to integrate a new vocal quality so quickly was unusual. Clients frequently tell me that shifting the way they speak feels inauthentic. In one way, that is true. The new vocal quality may not fit into the person's current identity, and that can be uncomfortable. After all, that identity wasn't constructed on purpose. It was cobbled together through a series of traumas, offhand comments, and cultural norms. It takes time and practice to stretch your sense of self to include a new vocal quality. The rewards of doing so, however, are well worth it. You gain the capacity to communicate with more flexibility and express more of your humanity. Authenticity isn't about staying fixed; it's about aligning with a wider truth. Sometimes finding your real voice means reclaiming what was once shamed or silenced.

Although all leaders are called upon to take on the role of healer at times, for some it is at the heart of their profession.

For them the Water voice becomes an essential element in doing their best work.

Here is a story about how one such leader found powerful ways to marshal his voice to transform palliative care for people at the end of life.

This physician was pursuing a postdoctoral fellowship in palliative care when he first contacted me. He decided to invest the wellness funds provided by his postdoctoral program to engage me as a voice coach. In his conversations with a mentor who had done voice coaching with me, he recognized that his voice was going to be an essential part of his success.

Our work commenced with a conversation about my client's vocal story, history, doubts, and aspirations. From there we familiarized him with each of the elements and their applications. He understood that the Water voice would be a powerful way to communicate with his patients and their families.

Like for most people, this physician's voice reflected his innate gifts. He was drawn to the healing work of palliative care because he was deeply committed to supporting people in having a good death. He already had easy access to his Water voice but wanted to increase his capacity to put it to use in his work.

One challenge was his grueling schedule of study and patient care. In our conversations about when and how to exercise his voice, I discovered that he had a strong commitment to daily spiritual practice. He began finishing his practice each morning with a Five Elements vocal warmup, some Water songs, and a poem. (I'll talk more about how song and poetry can support your vocal development later in this book.)

The physician began experimenting with speaking more intentionally with the Water voice. He immediately noticed that his patients relaxed and opened up more easily. Some of their conversations were still very difficult, but he felt confident that everyone involved knew they were being treated with care, compassion, and respect.

We also included some practices for building his Earth and Fire voice for when he needed to present his work and findings to groups of other physicians. In those settings, Earth and Fire enabled him to speak in a powerful, authoritative manner.

I was moved to hear how the Five Elements Framework enhanced his groundbreaking work. For many years I have been called to be present for the dying, both in my personal circle and as the founder and director of the Morning Star Singers, a volunteer choir that brings songs of comfort and healing to people facing illness and/or the end of life. Since we formed back in 2007, I have witnessed the power of song, sound, and loving presence to bring healing to people in challenging situations. It is a great honor to know that my approach to voice has become a powerful aspect of this physician's healing work.

Please go to www.barbaramcafee.com/full-voice-for-leaders to access guided Water voice exercises using several different characters. You'll also hear one of my songs, "Little One (Pema's Song)," a lullaby composed for a friend's little daughter on her first birthday.

After exploring these sounds, you may want to reflect on these questions:

What did you discover about your own Water voice?

Was the sound familiar, foreign, or somewhere in between?

How did it feel in your body?

Are there circumstances in your leadership setting that call for the caring, compassionate energy of Water?

Do you know people who embody this voice?

What qualities in them do you admire?

Feel free to pause and make some notes.

In working with the Water voice for all of these years, I've noticed something intriguing. The sound of weeping and the sound of comfort come from the same source: the Water voice. Many of us don't have access to our tears at all. We lost this deeply human capacity through a mixture of cultural norms, trauma, and/or shame. And I think that *is* a shame.

Those of us who still can cry often do so in utter silence, having been trained to stifle our expression of grief. That was my way for many years until I witnessed a woman in a therapy group giving full voice to her sobs. Her mouth was open. The sound was rich and throaty. My initial response of alarm and discomfort gave way to a yearning for that expression in my own body. Shortly thereafter, I found those sounds and have been crying out loud ever since.

Now we'll shift from the watery depths into the clarity of the Metal voice.

13

THE METAL VOICE: CUTTING THROUGH THE NOISE

Now it's time to sharpen your edges. Let's explore the bright, cutting clarity of the Metal voice: your built-in megaphone.

Here are some examples of Metal voices that you are likely to recognize:

A track and field coach instructs her runners at an outdoor practice: "OK, everybody, take another few laps to warm up."

Willie Nelson launches into his big hit "On the Road Again" for a crowd of cheering fans.

The Wicked Witch of the West screeches from the movie screen, "I'll fix you, my pretty, and your little dog too!"

A petulant child whines in the toy aisle, "But, Mom, I *want* it!"

Janice from the television show *Friends* delivers her classic line, "Oh, my *gawd*!"

A Siamese cat sends her piercing yowls echoing through the house in the wee hours.

Some other famous people who exemplify the Metal sound include Bob Dylan, Dolly Parton, Ralph Stanley, Cyndi Lauper, Neil Young, Pee-Wee Herman (Paul Rubens), Joan Rivers, and Steve Erkel from *Family Matters*. Can you think of others?

This bright, intense sound is sourced in your forehead, eyes, and nose area. It resonates in your sinus cavities, your body's amplification system. Metal is good for getting louder without vocal strain. It can also bring more clarity and focus both to your voice and to your thinking.

You can briefly sample the Metal voice by revisiting the character of a bratty child. Try saying "I'm a brat!" in your brattiest voice. Here's another opportunity to express some shadow. It's never too late to be a rotten kid. Try a few more, really leaning into it.

Now you may appreciate inhabiting this character or it may set your teeth on edge. If the latter is true, it doesn't necessarily mean that you hate the Metal voice. There are many characters that access each of these elements. Some of them will suit you better than others. We'll explore more Metal characters and practices later in this chapter.

The first iteration of the Five Elements Framework only included the elements of Earth, Fire, Water, and Air. That changed one day in a crowded restaurant. At the time I was hiding out in my Earth voice, not ready to be seen and heard in my true Fire. As you may recall, the Earth voice doesn't carry well, especially in a loud environment. My voice didn't reach across the teeny-tiny table, so my dining companion asked me multiple times to repeat myself. Then from across the room, I heard this voice. Sharp. Bright. Penetrating.

Clear as day, I heard a woman describing how her daughter hit the garage with her car and all that ensued thereafter. I looked for the source of this remarkable sound and discovered that she was at the complete opposite end of the restaurant. Somehow that voice cut through the background music, chattering patrons, and clattering dishes.

As I do when hear a voice, I tried to figure out where it fit into the elements. It wasn't Earth, Fire, Water, or Air. And then—*eureka!*—I thought of metal. Bright. Sharp. Able to cut through anything. The Metal voice was born. Now I can't imagine the framework without it. It's an essential human sound.

This element is a good choice if you are trying to project your voice in a loud, crowded place. It also comes in handy if you are talking with someone who really should get a hearing aid. As a longtime caregiver for my sweet mama, I made good use of the Metal voice in those times when she'd lost one of her hearing aids. The Metal voice made it possible for me to speak in way that she could hear me without straining my voice. Sometimes I'd forget to dial down the Metal when she'd get her replacement hearing aid. She'd start and put up her hands to quiet me down. Then we'd have a good laugh.

The Metal voice is a great ally in addressing vocal strain and fatigue. A facilitator who frequently leads three-day programs came to me with that exact issue. Every time she offered this training, she ended the three days with barely any voice and a very sore throat. Her default speaking voice was a mix of Earth and Water: grounded and warm. It worked very well for individual and small group conversations, but it didn't carry very well in a room full of people. Her message was getting lost. That meant her impact was too.

The Earth, Water, and Air voices can be "expensive." They often take a lot of air to make a sound. Metal, on the other hand, is the most efficient of the elements. It makes a lot of sound out of very little air.

My client was experiencing strain partly due to a lack of breath support. When she was focused and a little nervous, she would breathe more shallowly than usual. Most of us do. What little breath she had was insufficient to project her voice to edges of the room.

We waited for the facilitator's voice to recover and then got to work on some breathing exercises to increase the fuel for her voice. Then we turned to brightening up her sound with a bit of Metal. As usual, we began with an exaggerated version of the sound using characters like cats and witches. These outlandish versions of the Metal helped her get used to that buzzing, zingy feeling in her face. Then we worked to dial it back to a more reasonable scale, using text from her actual presentation.

She found a way to mix in enough of the Metal to make it effortless to speak with more volume. Just a small amount of that extra resonance, coupled with increased breath support, gave her significantly more vocal stamina. A little Metal goes a long way.

For many years I've said that the Metal voice is a great choice if your microphone dies. One of my clients, a rabbi at a large congregation, put that statement to a test.

This kind man had a Water voice that reflected his good heart. In addition to guiding his congregation, he was also a trusted leader in several national organizations. In many contexts his Water voice worked very well, but that vocal quality made it difficult for his aging congregants to hear him. We worked together in order to build more vocal strength and flexibility, focusing on Fire and Metal to help him project his voice.

In addition to vocal exercises, he built his Fire and Metal sounds by singing some swing jazz tunes he loved. In fact, he cooked up a special surprise for his wife on her birthday: a snazzy rendition of their love song, "Our Love Is Here to Stay." The singing helped him get used to sending more breath and energy through his voice. Then he could experiment with bringing that energy into how he was speaking.

Several months into our work together, his new sounds were put to the test during a High Holidays sermon. He was just starting one of his most important sermons of the year. The synagogue was packed to the rafters. Then—*clap, bang*—a thunderstorm knocked out power to his microphone. He immediately shifted to his Metal voice and stepped closer to the congregation. He proudly reported that even the people in the balcony were able to hear him just fine.

Another application of the Metal voice is to bring focus to a voice that is dull or monotonous. It's also a great antidote to mumbling. It can help improve diction by bringing the sound more forward: closer to the lips, tongue, and teeth, which shape your words and give them form. Some clients have also reported that speaking more clearly also helps them think more clearly.

The Metal voice has its downside as well. When I was first developing the framework, one of my organizational development colleagues referred a client to me for vocal coaching. This woman was a rising star in her organization with many leadership gifts to offer. The only problem? Her voice was pure Metal: harsh and shrill. That grating Metal sound created an insurmountable barrier to realizing her potential as a leader. How could she fully express her talents if nobody could stand to listen to her speak? I was moved by her predicament and did all I could to give her more vocal choices before she moved away to take a new position.

How many brilliant leaders like her are overlooked because of their vocal habits? What gifts are we missing because the person carrying them can't express them well? These are some the questions that drive my work with leaders.

Please go to www.barbaramcafee.com/full-voice-for-leaders to access guided Metal voice exercises using several different characters. You'll also hear the song "Caterpillar Stew," which exemplifies the Metal voice in song. It features my friend and cocomposer, Bruce O'Brien, on banjo, an instrument that brings a metallic twang to the song.

After exploring these sounds, you may wish to reflect on these questions:

What did you discover about your own Metal voice?

Was the sound familiar, foreign, or somewhere in between?

How did it feel in your body?

Are there circumstances in your leadership setting that call for the clear, focused energy of Metal? When have you needed to be heard and couldn't be? What kind of resonance might have made the difference?

Do you know people who embody this voice? What qualities in them do you admire?

You might like to pause and make some notes.

In my years of exploring this vocal quality in music as well as speaking, I've noticed something curious: people from mountainous regions frequently use the Metsl sound in their music. Metal is the dominant element in the music of the Balkan Mountains in southeastern Europe as well as bluegrass from the Appalachian Mountains in the southeastern United States. You can also hear it in yodeling from the Swiss Alps. My friend Linda was raised in the mountains of western North Carolina in a household that didn't have a car or telephone. If the family needed something from their neighbor across the valley, it was Linda's job to holler across the mountain. Their neighbor with the car would then come around to see what they needed. What element did Linda use to project her voice across the valley? Metal, of course.

We have one last element to explore: the Air voice.

14

THE AIR VOICE: AWAKENING THE IMAGINATION

Now it's time for us to catch the wind and take flight with the fifth and final element: Air.

Here are some examples of the Air voice you are likely to recognize:

A doting puppy parent gushes, "Who's a good boy? You're a good boy. Yes, you are!"

A storyteller at the fire draws in his listeners by leaning forward and casting a spell: "Once upon a time in a land far, far away . . ."

A mountain hiker comes over the ridge to behold a valley full of wildflowers and lets loose with a breathy "Wow!"

Glinda the Good Witch from *The Wizard of Oz* waves her wand and says, "Toto too!"

A baby squeals in delight as her grandparent babbles giddy nonsense.

Doves call in the hush of twilight.

Some famous people who exemplify the Air voice include Celtic singers like Enya, Jane Goodall, Smokey Robinson,

Billie Eilish, Mahatma Gandhi, Sabrina Carpenter, Pharrell Williams, Ruth Bader Ginsburg, and many Brazilian bossa nova singers. like Antonio Carlos Jobim. Can you think of others?

The Air voice is sourced in the crown of the head and even above it. It's the sound of a whisper, a sigh, a secret. Of all the elements, this one seems the least likely to be useful in a leadership setting. To many people. it feels too soft and vulnerable. It's true that the Air voice is not suitable for setting boundaries, giving clear direction, or asserting authority. But Air is the perfect choice for any number of work situations. including storytelling.

Storytelling can be a powerful skill for a leader to cultivate. A story can convey vision, build trust, deepen relationships, and open inspiration. I once coached the CEO of a wood products company to craft and vividly convey three key stories that most illustrated the organization's values. He shared these stories with every newly hired employee and often revisited them at key company events. At the outset of each telling, he'd shift out of his gruff Earth and Fire mix into an airy sound. It signaled to his listeners that a story was about to unfold, and they'd lean in closer to catch every word.

The Air voice can also be used to awaken new possibilities. You can be speaking in a normal tone of voice, but if you shift your tone to Air in order to say, "I have an idea," people will become curious and lean in. I sometimes think of the Air voice as a kind of time travel machine: it takes us from where we are now to the past in storytelling and to the future in sharing new possibilities. Air also awakens the imagination.

Let's open up the Air voice with a few delicious sighs. This sound is mostly breath, with just a shimmer of voice woven through. Feel the wind moving through your mouth as you take another delicious sigh. We'll explore more practices for opening the Air voice later in this chapter.

Just as the Earth voice can connect us to our gut instinct, I believe the Air voice connects us to the realm of spirit. Once again language demonstrates this connection. The words *spirit*, *inspiration*, and *respiration* are all derived from the Latin verb *spirare, to breathe.* This connection between air and spirit is expressed in many of the world's mystical traditions. In many indigenous cosmologies, wind is alive—a being, a messenger, a breath of the ancestors. Yogic traditions offer the breathing techniques of *pranayama*, where *prana* means *life force* and *yama* means *guiding* or *channeling.* In Judaism, one of the names for the divine is *ruach*: *wind*, *breath*, and *spirit* in one word. In Christian texts the Holy Spirit often arrives as a rushing wind. Across traditions, breath is not just air: it is presence and mystery.

I have firsthand experience with the link between the Air voice and the world of spirit.

Of all the elements, this was the one I disliked the most. But as I mentioned earlier in this book, the elements you hate are often the ones who have the greatest gifts for you. This was certainly the case for me.

I first befriended the Air voice through playing with a toddler friend. We created an ongoing game where we pretended to be poodles. I was "Boodle the Poodle" and he was "Boodle's" cousin, "Toodles." My poodle character was everything I wasn't. She was frivolous, fluffy, cute, and not too bright. And I loved pretending to be her, especially her airy, ditzy voice. It gave me a welcome break from being my tall, smart, and capable self.

Later, when I started accessing this sound with my voice teachers, I was surprised that it opened up so many tears. Why did these soft sounds affect me so deeply? As I continued my explorations of the Air voice, I recognized that it connected me to my childhood self and some of the pain I experienced during that time of my life. When we are small children, we speak in the Air voice. Everyone I know had to grow up way too fast. This sound can awaken the sense of vulnerability and innocence we have as children. This isn't the case for everyone, but I have witnessed the phenomenon in many of my clients over the years.

Getting more comfortable with the Air voice brought me much healing and also shifted some significant aspects of my life. I became more comfortable with being vulnerable. I lightened up. I even started moving and dressing differently. Most significantly, my sense of the sacred shifted to incorporate more of the feminine into my sense of the divine. Now I move between speech and song with Air in my voice, not as something I perform, but as something that belongs to me as naturally as breath itself. I am grateful for the many gifts that came with welcoming this part of me back home. I can't imagine living without the blessings of the Air voice.

Have you noticed a recurring pattern in the stories I've been sharing? Over and over I have witnessed how cultivating one's full voice often brings unexpected gifts into my clients' lives. It makes sense: when your voice is more alive, other aspects of your life—your physical body, facial expressions, emotions, intentions, relationships, and gifts—can't help but come alive as well.

I often encounter the Air sound among emerging women leaders: their voices gentle, tentative, and sometimes under-supported. They may have naturally soft voices, or they may have ended up speaking quietly out of a lack of confidence or shyness. Gender norms may come into play as well. In any case, their contributions are often overlooked or dismissed by their colleagues.

One of these women, the executive director of a large non-profit, was sent to my voice coaching practice by her board of directors. Her performance review revealed strength after strength, with one exception: her voice. Her position required her to interact frequently with the media. In television and radio interviews, this brilliant woman sounded young and insecure. She spoke quickly, with a very airy tone, with vocal fry. It didn't reflect well on her, her organization, or their worthy mission. She recognized the truth of what her colleagues were telling her; she just didn't know how to change it on her own.

Let me take a quick aside to address *vocal fry*. You've probably heard vocal fry even if you don't know what it is. It sounds like popping or sizzling and is caused by the vocal cords closing so that only a few bubbles of air can get through. I think of it as a kind of "breath anorexia." This phenomenon has become increasingly common, especially among people under forty. Although it doesn't injure your voice, it can put off your listeners. I heard one person describe it as the vocal equivalent of dragging your feet. Sometimes vocal fry happens naturally when you are exhausted. If you use it in your everyday conversation, you'll sound tired even if you aren't. Vocal fry can diminish your authority and credibility and make it difficult to hear you.

My work with my client focused on several things: grounding her sound in her body through the elements of Earth and Fire, slowing down her rate of speaking, and improving her breath support. In this process, she made some intriguing discoveries about why she talked the way she did. Many of them resulted from her early professional experiences.

In a previous position, she had a fairly common experience for women: struggling to make her voice heard among a predominantly male team. She would offer an idea and get no response. A few minutes later a man would make the same suggestion and receive enthusiastic support. In this setting, she also experienced frequent interruptions and other messages that her voice was not valued. Over time she attempted to compensate by speaking more quickly and trying to lower her voice to a more masculine range. The tension also caused her to breathe more shallowly.

We worked with reciting poetry as a way to fuel her voice with breath, practice using clear tone, and slow down. This exploration of eloquent speech helped her integrate her new habits in her everyday speech. (I'll explore voice and gender in more depth in the next chapter.)

As I've mentioned before, someone's tone of voice can often point to their gifts. If I hear someone with an Air voice, I ask them if they are the people who can see the future before anyone else. They generally say yes, with a smile. (It feels good to be seen.) This same vocal quality that can be a detriment to being taken seriously can also be used intentionally to create a sense of wonder and curiosity. In fact, when we see something amazing in the world, like a rainbow, many of us respond by taking in a deep breath and sighing out, "Wow!"

Please go to www.barbaramcafee.com/full-voice-for-leaders to access guided Air voice exercises using several different characters. You'll also hear one of my songs, "Breathing Trees," which exemplifies the Air voice in song and celebrates our symbiotic relationship with our ancient relatives, the trees.

After exploring these sounds, reflect on these questions:

What did you discover about your own Air voice?

Was the sound familiar, foreign, or somewhere in between?

How did it feel in your body?

Where in your leadership are you called to awaken your colleagues' imaginations about new possibilities?

What stories would you like to craft in support of your leadership?

What inspires you about the work you do, and how do you want to share that with the people around you?

Do you know people who embody this voice? What qualities in them do you admire?

Feel free to pause and make some notes.

Now that you've gotten a taste of all five elements, let's investigate how gender affects voice.

15

VOICE, GENDER, AND THE ALCHEMY OF WHOLENESS

The social constructs of gender have been undergoing profound shifts in recent decades. What was once widely framed as a fixed binary—male/female—is now increasingly understood as a complex, evolving spectrum of identities, expressions, and lived experiences. At the same time, many enduring norms around "masculine" and "feminine" behaviors still shape how people are treated and how we learn to use (or suppress) our voices. From birth onward, families, schools, media, clothing, and toys enforce these norms, often in ways that are invisible until they are challenged.

No matter what your gender identity or history, reclaiming both expressive and receptive capacities across the full spectrum of vocal elements can bring you closer to an embodied sense of wholeness. Voice becomes not just a tool for communication, but a portal to reconnect with long-silenced parts of yourself and to transform cultural residue into creative agency.

I'm going to talk about people who are raised as women first and then about people raised as men. I'll be sharing what I've discovered from working with my clients over the years.

People raised as women are often flooded with expectations to be nice, nurturing, sweet, accommodating, and gentle—what dominant culture deems "feminine." These social cues often nudge women toward using Water and Air voices while discouraging Fire and Metal. Some internalize these messages deeply. Others resist, sometimes by abandoning the very qualities (care, compassion, receptivity) that in a different context might be wielded as strengths. Many do both, adapting their vocal expression moment by moment in complex, unconscious ways.

Despite their best efforts, women face particular communication challenges:

The dominant norm for leadership is male.

Anger is often interpreted as hysteria.

Assertiveness is often viewed as bossiness.

Brilliance is met with "mansplaining."

Women leaders are interrupted even at the highest levels of society. One study of the U.S. Supreme Court found that female justices were interrupted 108 percent more often than their male colleagues between 2009 and 2018.

In recent history, there is some movement in welcoming more diversity in expressing femininity. Even so, the long history of sexism is still at work in all of us.

At a deeper level, many women come to distrust their own voices, not only in the literal sense of speaking, but also in their inner compass, their gut, their intuitive knowing.

This distrust isn't just personal, it's ancestral. Centuries of silencing live in our cells. So do the longings of foremothers whose voices were never heard, whose rage and brilliance were buried under propriety. Some of us carry their grief. Others carry their rebellion. Often we carry both.

I have several female ancestors who rejected that silencing. I can feel their influence on my own voice. One of them was my maternal grandmother, Norma Mershon Mathis. She was born in 1901 and was in college when women got the vote in the United States. That event shaped the rest of her life. She was passionate about politics and held a number of positions in civic life before becoming the executive secretary to the governor of Iowa in the 1950s. During that era, she most likely had to align herself with a man to gain any power or influence. I can't imagine her grief when the governor and his wife were killed in a car accident. Besides losing two dear friends, she lost a job she passionately loved.

Grandma died when I was seventeen, so I never got to talk with her about her life. I am grateful for her example as I live my own life of independence and contribution. And I can't believe that in my own lifetime I've known so many people who were alive before women had the right to their political voice in the United States. I'm also aware of my sisters around the world whose voices continue to be suppressed by poverty, war, disease, hunger, and the lack of basic human rights.

Many of the powerful women I work with in my voice coaching practice have felt the need to excise or downplay more traditionally feminine qualities (and voices) when they work in male-dominated fields and organizations. They get the message early on that they can't afford to be soft. Many of them speak in lower voices than their natural tone in order to be taken seriously. These strategies may make them more effective in their day-to-day work, but they often come at a high personal cost.

One of my clients worked as the medical director for a large hospital. She was the first woman in that position and the only woman at the table full of men. In order to build her credibility with her male colleagues, she unconsciously modified her speaking voice to express more Earth. After many years in this role, she shifted her work away from hospital leadership into a mix of patient care and community work. She came to work with me initially to reclaim her singing voice. With the constant lowering of her voice, she'd lost some of her upper singing range.

As she opened up her voice, she came to realize that she'd lost more than her high notes: she'd lost touch with many cherished aspects of herself as a woman. One of those qualities she was ready to reclaim was her wildness. She had spent so many years being impeccable, strong, and smart that she was ready to play with the archetype of the "bad girl."

We found her a few "red dress songs": bluesy tunes full of sass and double entendres. These sexy songs inspired her to go to a consignment store to buy herself a red dress. As far as I know, she never wore it out in public, only when she wanted to sing her wild song and reinhabit her bold and brassy self. Her red dress became more than a costume. It was a ritual object: a thread back to a self she had tucked away for decades. As she reinhabited her voice—sass, sensuality, vibrato, and all—she also reinhabited a more playful, liberated version of herself. The high notes she'd lost weren't just musical; they were emotional, even spiritual. And she was ready to sing them again.

I wish we lived in a world where all voices were welcome, where clarity didn't require strain, and where softness wasn't mistaken for weakness. That world may not be fully here yet. But every time we reclaim a part of our own voice, whether Water or Fire, wildness or wonder, we plant a seed. The work is not to perform over culture's noise, but to reclaim our voices from the inside out. This is how we grow into self-trust. This is how we build the future—one full, whole, liberated voice at a time.

Some inspiring, trailblazing women have bucked the feminine norms in powerful ways. Here are a few of them:

Andrea Gibson: the proudly nonbinary poet laureate of Colorado

Whoopi Goldberg: a voice completely earthy and sly

Janis Joplin: a blend of Fire and gravel without apology

Kathleen Turner: deep, deep, deep

Eartha Kitt: a mix between a purr and a meow with shivers added

k.d. lang: a smooth blend of satin, smoke, and grit

Now let's turn toward another deeply patterned pathway: the one navigated by those raised as boys and men. While the specific pressures differ, the constriction is no less real and often no less painful. Instead of being told to stay soft, boys are told to be hard. Instead of being taught to accommodate, they're expected to dominate. They are trained out of tenderness, out of wonder, out of tears. What does that do to a voice?

People who are raised as men get powerful messages about how they should be: strong, stoic, competitive, and assertive. These qualities all congeal in the macho stereotype. These ideas about masculinity are enforced through unkind teasing, violence, or the threat of it. It is dangerous to be feminine as a man or boy. If you show any signs of it, you may be perceived as gay and can be hurt or killed.

The dominant culture often tells boys that to be a "real man" is to be emotionally dead—in the face, in the voice, and in the body. They learn to trade fluidity for rigidity, connection for control, and aliveness for approval.

There are many exceptions to this message in various subcultures, but the heroes we see in movies and stories reflect this emotional numbness: stoic, silent, often more machine than man. Think of the Terminator, Batman, and the Mandalorian. What are we saying when our icons of masculine power are armored, masked, and expressionless? What are we teaching when vulnerability is only permitted in death scenes?

As a result, many of the men I work with are stuck in a narrow, flat vocal range that is often lower than where their voices would naturally be. Their faces and bodies can become immobile and inexpressive. These habits can be limiting to their effectiveness as leaders, because they hinder their ability to make authentic connections with others. More importantly, these habits stifle their own sense of aliveness.

Stretching their expression in order to become more alive in their faces and bodies can require bravery in men and sometimes leads to deep healing. Using archetypes and characters can make it safe enough to step beyond socially approved boundaries. I have also witnessed many men weeping healing tears when they finally open their voices, bodies, and psyches to welcome their softer side with a tender love song or lullaby.

Some well-known men have expanded the realm of emotional expression for men. For example:

Fred Rogers: for his gentleness and emotional literacy

Prince: for how he bent gender norms in pioneering ways with a voice that traveled every realm

Barack Obama: for his deliberate calm mixed with emotional authenticity

Lin-Manuel Miranda: for his playful, dynamic expressiveness

Jason Momoa: for his counter-stereotype of masculinity that includes joy, affection, and tears

Harry Styles: for his soft voice, androgynous style, and refusal to play by old masculine rules

I also want to give a nod here to the beautiful queer icons who help stretch the boundaries of gender: people like Elton John, George Michael, Billy Porter, Alok Vaid-Menon, Boy George, Lil Nas X, and Cole Escola.

I remember when I first understood in my bones how narrow the accepted range of expression is for men. I was training a group of leaders at an engineering firm. They were committed to creating a workplace that welcomed and supported the whole person. As a group of introverted leaders, they recognized the need to expand the way they communicated with their team members and colleagues in order to achieve that goal.

When we were exploring the Water element, I had them close their eyes and sway while making warm "oo" sounds. As I looked at them in that tender moment, it struck me that all the things they were striving to become—compassionate, supportive, welcoming—were antithetical to masculine socialization. I shared this insight with them and suggested that they might experience some internalized homophobia when they expanded beyond their usual way of speaking. I asked them to commit *never* to tease another man for being too expressive, emotional, and alive. They agreed.

The whole time I was talking in this unplanned way, I was wondering how this conversation was landing with the founder of the firm, a former Marine. After the session, he came up full of enthusiasm and suggested that I bring the work to the Marine Corps leadership training in Quantico, Virginia. I guess he liked it, and no, that hasn't happened. Yet.

I've had the privilege of working with a few trans clients over the years, though I'm aware that there are now skilled voice coaches who specialize in supporting them through the nuanced vocal transitions that often accompany medical or social gender affirmation.

One trans woman I worked with shared a specific and heartfelt goal: to be "ma'am-ed" at the McDonald's drive-through. This desire wasn't trivial. It was about recognition, safety, and belonging. Through focused practice in her Air and Water voices, she eventually succeeded. I've rarely seen such radiant joy in a voice coaching session.

In conversations with other trans friends in the singing community, I have witnessed how necessary it is to incorporate work with voice as they transition. It can be especially challenging for trans women, because their vocal cords don't change much with hormone treatments. Their voice work needs to incorporate the thicker cords that were formed by testosterone. Trans men, however, do experience significant vocal shifts as their hormone treatments thicken up the vocal cords.

No matter what your gender identity, I invite you to inhabit all of your sounds—the ones that are familiar and unfamiliar, the ones that are socially acceptable and the ones that run counter to polite society. I guarantee it will support you in leading from a place of wholeness, self-awareness, and flexibility.

16

INTEGRATION AND ARCHETYPES

We've traveled far together, from delving into how voice touches our lives to your own vocal autobiography to exploring all five elements. Take a moment: what are you noticing now in the way you speak, the way you listen, the way your voice meets the world?

Here is one common question I encounter after people have the chance to try out the exaggerated and sometimes silly versions of the elements: "How do I bring what I've discovered from playing with my voice into how I talk every day?" The next portion of this book guides you through some exercises and suggestions for doing just that.

To begin the process, you'll consider how much access you have to each element.

For Earth, Fire, Water, Metal, and Air, rate yourself from one to five, one being not much access at all and five being very strong. Then write a little about your associations with that element. You might even jot down examples of when each element appears—or hides—in your daily speech.

Please note that most of us use a mixture of two elements in our everyday speaking voice. Don't worry about getting it right. The inquiry is at least as valuable as the answer.

Now select two elements that you most want to develop, either because you don't have access to them or because the qualities they express would be useful in your life.

To ground yourself into calm authority and gut instinct, choose Earth.

To kindle more passion and become more vibrant and visible, choose Fire.

To awaken more caring, empathy, and heart, choose Water.

To sharpen your clarity and make yourself heard, choose Metal.

To breathe life into awe and imagination, choose Air.

Next I'll guide you in choosing archetypes that will support you in accessing these elements in your voice and your leadership. In the Five Elements practices, you made use of archetypes to open up new sounds in your voice. Now we'll discover how to engage them as allies for your leadership voice.

King Richard II in William Shakespeare's play of the same name says, "Thus play I in one person many people." Much of what we've done so far is to open up more possibilities in your story about yourself. I hope you are noticing the ways that you, like Richard II, play many distinct roles in your life and how each one affects your voice.

Life is mythological. Underneath the ordinary events of our days lies a deeper pattern. To quote Shakespeare again: "All the world's a stage, / And all the men and women merely players; / They have their exits and their entrances; / And one man in his time plays many parts."

As you consider your stage, what characters are you playing? Are you a disruptor? A magician? A workhorse? A seer of the future? an unsung hero?

Consider also the play in which you are operating. What is the overarching drama that is unfolding in your organization? Are you in a rapid ascent full of optimism and energy? In a holding pattern waiting and waiting for something to shift? In a cycle of diminishment and ending?

As you have seen in the Five Elements exercises, there is great power in stepping beyond the personal and into the archetypal. The challenges that surround you become less particular to your story and instead reflect the great themes of humankind. Conundrums that perplex you now most likely echo the struggles of the people who came before you—and they are certainly shared by many other leaders at this moment.

For most of human existence on earth, archetypes have been an integral part of people's lives. In many indigenous cultures, they still are. It's only recently that most of us in the Western world have abandoned this relationship with the unseen. I am convinced that these powerful energies are still here and ready to support us. Of course, I can't prove any of this scientifically, but as my friend and mentor Peter Block says: "I don't know if it's true, but it's useful."

Some examples of archetypes that recur in cultures around the world include ruler, sage, catalyst, wizard or witch, visionary, hero or heroine, nurturer, teacher, and jester. These characters show up in myths, legends, and fairy tales throughout time as well as in many contemporary films.

Before I invite you to consider your archetypal allies, let me introduce you to my own. When I am teaching or doing a presentation, the archetypes I call upon are the High Priestess and the Holy Fool. The High Priestess supports the sacred work of calling people into their full expression. At the same time, my approach to that work requires play and silliness. When I'm embodying the Holy Fool, it creates space for others to be more playful as well. Although these archetypes influence the way I speak, I consider them when I'm crafting the flow of my presentations. They also affect what I wear and how I move.

Feel free to consider the archetypes that will be most useful to you at this time. Just to review a few of the options: ruler, sage, catalyst, wizard or witch, rebel, visionary, hero or heroine, truth teller, nurturer, teacher, and jester. You can also find many lists of archetypes, mythical characters, gods, and goddesses on the Internet. Enjoy musing on this question and notice what arises as you do.

Archetypes don't just live in legend; they walk beside us in the voices we admire. You can also draw on real people to inspire your vocal expansion. Is there someone whose voice exemplifies the qualities you are seeking to develop in your own? You can experiment with bringing some of their qualities into your speech.

For instance, I call on two powerful women to influence my voice. When I want to access more gravitas and dignity, I call on the late Maya Angelou, who was a prolific poet, author, activist, actor, and director. Her gracious and eloquent way of speaking grounds me in all of the right ways. I slow down. I feel the Earth voice humming like a cello in my chest. Angelou helps me stand tall. I've been unusually tall all of my life. For many years, that height made me feel awkward, clumsy, and out of sync with how I was supposed to be as a girl. Angelou was around my same height and carried herself like the dancer she was. When I think of her, I carry myself with some of her grace and elegance.

I also refer to my friend, author and teacher Dr. Margaret Wheatley in this way. I'm very familiar with Meg's voice because we've worked together extensively. She and I collaborated on the thirteen-city Women's Leadership Revival tour. Like an old-time tent revival, we traveled to North American cities to catalyze women's leadership. She was the speaker; I was the band and also wrote the anthem for the tour. I call upon the memory of Meg's voice to help me speak more clearly and deliberately. Even now, when I feel myself rushing or rambling, I summon the rhythm of her cadence, and it brings me home.

As you consider the elements you want to cultivate in your voice, are there specific people who exemplify those qualities?

Are there people whose voices inspire you?

Is it possible to bring some of their vocal qualities into how you speak?

Feel free to pause while you consider this question and experiment with integrating these sounds into your own voice. Trying on new vocal qualities can feel like playing dress-up with a stranger's clothes. That's normal. Try it anyway.

Your imagination is powerful. Calling forth these iconic energies can provide a bridge to fuller expression. I encourage you to practice embodying, and giving voice to, these archetypes in your everyday life. They will enrich the way you speak with new sounds and will connect you to the broader pattern of which we are all a part.

17

SINGING AS A BRIDGE: WEAVING SOUND INTO SPEECH

There is a sound that lives just beyond speech. It's the realm of singing. Not for performance, not for praise, but for your own resonance and remembering.

Another way to bring the Five Elements into your speaking voice is through singing. As I've mentioned before, singing is a natural way to bring what you find in the expansive realms of sound closer to how you express yourself every day. Singing is the bridge between sound and speech.

Many of us carry a limiting story about singing. Perhaps someone told you that you were tone-deaf when you were young. (By the way, only 4 percent of people are truly tone-deaf.) Maybe you think you should sound like a famous recording artist before you even dare to open your mouth. Whatever barriers arise when you consider singing, I invite you to bravely step beyond them. This isn't about quitting your day job to become a famous rock and roll singer or opera diva. (Although who knows what might happen when you open your full voice?) I can guarantee that singing will support you in bringing more breath, energy, and aliveness into the way you speak.

When you look closely, singing isn't that different from speaking. You use the exact same mechanisms for the two activities. Breath moves across the vocal cords. They vibrate and resonate in the sinus cavities. Lips, tongue, and teeth form words. Singing is just slow, structured speech that incorporates more variation in range and volume. That's it from a physical point of view.

When we dig a little deeper, we discover that singing does wonders for your voice and expression. To begin with singing requires much more breath than speaking. Thus you build your capacity to fuel your voice with a steady flow of air. It incorporates more range and color in your sound, which helps you expand your vocal flexibility. Singing helps you feel your own sound moving through the body. Singing amplifies your movements and facial expressions. It allows you to practice incorporating more physical energy into how you speak.

A song is an avenue for tapping into powerful emotions as well. Just by singing a song, you can calm your nervous system or ramp up your energy or metabolize your grief. A song can carry you back in time, shift your mood, or kindle a connection to mystery. Your ancestors knew this well.

Songs are also trusty mnemonic devices for remembering how to access the elements. You may be vague about how to access your Earth voice, but singing along with Johnny Cash or Tracy Chapman will help you remember. Singing along with Bruce Springsteen or Tina Turner will open up your Fire instantly. Willie Nelson, Lucinda Williams, and

Dolly Parton can be your guides to tapping into the twang of Metal. The Air voice may be elusive until you sing along with Enya, Billie Eilish, or Smokey Robinson.

Recently I worked with a psychologist who has been making use of singing in her vocal development. As part of her work, she teaches online psychology courses. After receiving negative feedback about her voice, she contacted me for voice coaching. The evaluations mentioned that her voice sounded immature, hesitant, and difficult to hear. She also used a distracting number of "um's" and "ah's."

Her speaking voice is naturally light and relatively high. She is an introverted person who works primarily one-on-one with clients, so these qualities have been reinforced. When we first opened up all five elements in her voice, I was astonished to discover that she was able to go extremely low in her Earth voice. None of that sound is evident in how she speaks. Whenever a client has an exceptional aspect to their voice like this, I let them know that they have a gift. We've yet to uncover the significance of my client's unusual Earth voice, but she is happy to know that she has such a solid foundation under her soft voice.

In our work together she has been practicing a number of songs. They are all by artists she admires and express sentiments that align with her own. Singing has strengthened her voice. She speaks with more ease and vibrancy. Perhaps most importantly, she has become accustomed to taking up more physical and sonic space. She sounds more confident because she *is* more confident.

Recently she brought some wonderful affirmation of her diligent voice work. Her evaluations from a recent training were full of positive feedback and made no mention of her previous voice issues.

You can continue practicing all of the Five Elements by singing simple songs that evoke them. One way to bring more singing into your everyday life is to make what I call "an irresistible playlist": a variety pack of songs you love that invite you into different vocal sounds. This playlist serves as a good workout for your voice. You can sing along to it in the car or while cooking dinner. If you love the songs, you'll find a time and place to sing them.

Here are a few suggestions for gathering songs that evoke each element.

For Earth, I suggest African American spirituals like "Sometimes I Feel Like a Motherless Child," Johnny Cash's "Ring of Fire," "Summertime," "We Shall Overcome," laments, or slow blues.

For Fire, try "I Feel Good" by James Brown, "Oh, What a Beautiful Morning" from the musical *Oklahoma*, "This Little Light of Mine," or any song by your favorite rocker or Broadway belter.

For Water, choose songs like "Moon River," John Lennon's "Imagine," "Shenandoah," "The Sound of Music," or flowing romantic ballads.

Metal voice songs could include Patsy Cline's "Crazy," "I'll Fly Away," "Blue Skies" by Willie Nelson, "Jolene" by Dolly Parton, "Girls Just Wanna Have Fun" by Cyndi Lauper, as well as bluegrass or country songs.

For Air, I suggest "Edelweiss" from *The Sound of Music*, "Fields of Gold" by Sting, "Blackbird," "Dream a Little Dream of Me," and "Twinkle, Twinkle, Little Star."

Here's some great news: there are karaoke tracks for many popular songs. Once you learn a song by singing along with the artist, you can get the karaoke track and become the soloist yourself—even in your pajamas, even in your kitchen. No stage required.

Another way to invite song into your day-to-day life is to gather songs for specific occasions, such as:

Greeting the day
Blessing a meal
Offering solace to someone who is grieving or ill
Bidding farewell
Celebrating the seasons
Singing a precious one to sleep
Invoking the sacred

You probably know more songs, or parts of songs, than you think. Once you start seeking out songs, you will start remembering the ones you know: songs from childhood and camp, songs from places of worship, pop songs you loved as a teenager, and movie themes. I suggest keeping a running list on your phone of the ones you especially like.

Over the years I have witnessed many clients reclaim singing as part of their everyday lives, sometimes with surprising results. One led his team in learning a round together as an experiment in listening. Others have polished up a particularly meaningful tune to share as a gift for a loved one. A therapist created a list of songs to have on hand for singing to his clients in difficult moments. And more than one has learned songs to support a beloved friend or family member at the end of life. One of my early clients said this after learning a lullaby for his future children: "Barbara, singing is a human right."

What songs have followed you through the years?

Which ones make you feel most like yourself?

Pause to write down the songs you may want to sing.

As you say yes to singing, let your voice stumble, shimmer, crack, and fly. Let it carry you, not toward perfection, but toward aliveness. This is the sound just beyond speech. Let it live in you.

18

PRACTICING POETRY: A PATHWAY TO ELOQUENT SPEECH

Consider for a moment how long there were human beings before the advent of the written word. A common estimate is 200,000 years. That's 200,000 years of transmitting everything from one generation to the next through the oral tradition—everything from creation myths and hunting methods to key ceremonies, family lineages, and which mushrooms are likely to kill you.

When words are structured in song or poetry, they are more easily remembered. That's why there is such a long tradition of recitation around the world.

In Mesopotamia, Egypt, India, Greece, and beyond, bards and oral storytellers performed epic poems and myths like Homer's *Iliad* and *Odyssey* or the Vedic hymns of India. Native cultures of Australia, New Zealand, and North America relied on the spoken word to transmit important moral and spiritual messages.

The Psalms and Biblical poetry have been recited in the Jewish and Christian traditions for millennia.

The poetry of the Chinese Tang Dynasty is often memorized and recited in schools.

In West Africa, griots, traditional storytellers and musicians, transmit ancestral narratives through a blend of poetry, music, song, and dance.

In Islamic tradition, a *hafiẓ* is someone who has committed the entire Qur'an to memory: a feat of devotion, discipline, and oral mastery.

In medieval Europe, the traveling troubadours and minstrels carried poems of courtly love, chivalry, and local legends from place to place.

These traditions are the forerunners of the slam poetry movement dating back to the 1980s. These poets express personal and political themes in vibrant, rhythmic recitations.

Now you have an opportunity to step into this river of poetry as a way to practice more eloquent, embodied speech. Poetry lives in the liminal space between song and everyday conversation. It asks something different of us—something slower and more deliberate. You wouldn't recite a poem as you would order a latte or rattle off a to-do list. Poetry asks you to slow down, to savor. It's the art of speaking soulfully.

Poems express their ideas in unusual ways that require more processing time. This purposeful way of speaking is good practice for those of us who tend to speak too quickly. We may be able to say lots and lots of words in a short amount of time, but their deeper meaning can get lost along the way.

Poetry can also invite us to bring more pleasure into how we are speaking, to taste the words as they are coming out of our mouths. When we take more pleasure in speaking, the people listening to us will catch that pleasure, and they will hear us more deeply than if we are rambling along without paying attention.

Now I'll explain some ways to work with poetry using the Five Elements. First find a poem to explore. If you can, choose one you love.

If you don't know poetry, here are a few suggestions that are easy to find on the Internet. I suggest printing out a paper copy of the poem you choose.

"The Peace of Wild Things" by Wendell Berry

"Wild Geese" by Mary Oliver

"Blessing the Boats at St. Mary's" by Lucille Clifton

"The Guesthouse" by Jelaluddin Rumi

"The Thread" by William Stafford

"Wayfarer" by Antonio Machado

"Kindness" by Naomi Shihab Nye

Once you've found your poem, find a place where you are able to speak comfortably out loud.

Read the poem aloud several times slowly and clearly, just to hear yourself speak it and to sense the meaning. I suggest recording one of these early renditions so you can track how it changes as you work with it.

Notice what shifts in your breath, posture, and pace when you enter poetic language.

What happens when words carry rhythm and reverence?

Experience any images or sensations vividly with all of your senses.

See, hear, taste, touch, and smell what the words evoke.

Pay attention to how your mouth forms each word and how those words connect to each other.

Let your voice shift in response to the words.

Let it get louder, softer, higher, and lower.

Let it ripple with meaning.

Enjoy the "song" unfolding from the words.

Consider the emotional tone of the poem and experiment with using the elements to help convey that.

As you continue to work with the poem, notice how your voice is the same as or different from how you normally speak. Are there qualities you'd like to invite into your speech?

Try reading the poem a few times as though your listener doesn't speak your language. How might you carry the meaning with only breath, tone, and gesture, without relying on the words themselves?

If possible, try memorizing the poem or at least a portion of it. How does getting free of the paper shift how you speak it?

What did you discover in this experiment?

Are there elements you want to integrate into your everyday speaking voice?

Feel free to pause to make some notes.

If you enjoy poetry, I suggest memorizing a few of your favorites. I've discovered that I memorize a poem more easily by listening to a recording of it rather than reading it off a page. You can record yourself reading the poem and practice it while walking or driving. I used to memorize poems by listening to recordings through earbuds on the busy Minneapolis walking paths. At first, I felt foolish walking down the street talking to myself. Then I realized that I just looked like someone talking on the phone. It set me free.

It is a joy to have just the right poem available when you need it. A number of the leaders I've coached over the years have so enjoyed working with poetry that they have integrated an opening and/or closing poem into their team meetings. Others keep a file of their favorites on hand to use in presentations and speeches. Even if you never bring them into your work, poems can become lifelong companions. They awaken new colors in your voice and tend the soul with their beauty.

Another favorite poet of mine, Theodore Roethke, said, "May my silences become more accurate."

As you practice more poetic speech, may your silences hold as much beauty as your sounds.

19

LIVING THE FIVE ELEMENTS: EVERYDAY PRACTICES FOR VOCAL PRESENCE

You've howled, whispered, cackled, and crooned.

You've summoned archetypes, sung lullabies, and tasted poems aloud.

Now comes the real magic: weaving these elemental voices into everyday conversation. There are four primary practices for doing this:

1. **Noticing, noticing, noticing.** Notice the ways your voice shifts in different situations.

How does it shift with different people?

Do you shift it intentionally or automatically?

You can also tune in to the voices around you. What element is your colleague using during that tense meeting? What does the barista's tone reveal about her morning?

2. **Exercising your full voice.** Maintaining and expanding your vocal choices requires practice, much like a yoga or fitness routine.

A simple way to visit all five voices in a short period of time is through laughter.

Earth: Santa Claus (ho, ho, ho)

Fire: a brash comedian (ha, ha, ha)

Water: a giddy British matron (hoo, hoo, hoo)

Metal: a cackling witch

Air: a ticklish baby (hee, hee, hee)

This practice may also offer a side benefit of cheering you up!

Here is another quick warm-up that works and delights: a vocal parade using characters from the *Wizard of Oz* movie:

Earth: the flying monkeys' chant as they march into the witch's castle ("oh ee oh, oh-oh")

Fire: the wizard as he operates his fancy machine ("Pay no attention to that man behind the curtain!")

Water: Dorothy singing the first few lines of "Over the Rainbow"

Metal: the Wicked Witch of the West threatening Dorothy ("I'll fix you, my pretty, and your little dog too!")

Air: Glinda the Good Witch ("Toto too!")

Remember that you can access exercises and a song for each element at www.barbaramcafee.com/full-voice-for-leaders.

You can exercise more of your full range through singing and poetry, as I described earlier.

Even if you don't have young children in your life, reading children's books out loud is a wonderful way to exercise more expressive speech.

3. **Experimentation.** As you prepare to talk with an individual or group, consider which element or elements will best support your message. Reflect not only on what you want to say, but on how you want to say it and which voice will carry it best.

If you are preparing a speech or presentation, you can apply the poetry process we've just explored to your text. Identify which parts of your presentation require gravitas (Earth) and which ones may flourish with some passion (Fire). Are you stepping into a moment of vulnerability (Water), or is it time to make a clear and incisive point (Metal)? When will you share an inspiring story (Air)?

As you practice, feel free to exaggerate these sounds to get used to inhabiting more vocal variation. You can back them off to something more reasonable when you are actually doing your presentation.

By now you have access to a broader variety of vocal choices, so if how you are speaking isn't connecting with your listeners, you'll be able to shift your tone until you make a connection with them. You probably know when you're losing your audience. It's an awful feeling. In that circumstance, most of persist in what's not working. Having access to the elements helps you shift with agility. You're no longer stuck in a default setting; you have tools to pivot, reconnect, and reenchant.

4. **Finally, don't keep this to yourself.** Share the Five Elements with your colleagues and family members.

A simple way to do so is to share my TEDx talk called "Bringing Your Full Voice to Life." You may also share this book with them. Sharing a common language to talk about voice can offer rich opportunities for coaching each other on more effective communication.

And the Five Elements Framework sticks with people over the long term. For over a decade, a professor at a university in the southeastern United States has been assigning my first book, *Full Voice: The Art and Practice of Vocal Presence*, to students in his interdisciplinary leadership course. He recently told me that students still refer to the elements when they get in touch with him many years after graduating.

As a leader, you spend much of your day speaking and listening. Each interaction offers you the opportunity to engage the five elements in creating more powerful and effective communication.

You already carry all five elements in you.

Let your voice become the place where they meet.

Speak with Earth's steadiness, Fire's conviction, Water's care, Metal's clarity, and Air's wonder.

Your voice is not just a tool: it's a way of being.

20

CIRCLING BACK

One ancestor of this work, Alfred Wolfsohn—the World War I veteran whose suffering and recovery shaped a radical approach to the human voice—once said: "The voice is the muscle of the soul."

What a profound statement! If the soul could flex, could stretch, could tremble with aliveness, I wonder if it would sound something like the voice you've been discovering.

{PART THREE}

Who Are You Going to Be While You Do What You Do?

21

FIVE PRACTICES TO SUSTAIN YOUR BEING

We've journeyed together through the terrain of voice: its elements, its archetypes, its playfulness and power. Now, as we enter the final stretch of this book, we shift focus from how you speak to how you *be*.

Consider this your parting bouquet: five soul-rooted practices to help you stay whole in a world that often rewards fragmentation. Practices for returning to yourself again and again in the midst of leadership and living.

These practices are not novel. They have been carried across time in many traditions. You may recognize them. I offer them not as instruction, but as invitation: a gentle nudge to reclaim what you know in your bones.

Each practice correlates with a finger, so feel free to pause in order to take a piece of paper and draw an outline your hand. You can use this paper to take notes on what you want to remember and hang it somewhere as a touchstone for these ideas.

Each practice arrives wrapped in story, song, poetry, and/or a few words from wise companions who have walked ahead of us, made their mistakes, and left behind glimmers of guidance.

Let's begin with the late Thomas Merton, Trappist monk and fierce champion of the inner life. He wrote: "We are so obsessed with doing that we have no time and no imagination left for being. As a result, we are valued not for what we are but for what we do or what we have—for our usefulness."

Leadership, in any form, asks us to show up with presence, resilience, curiosity, and care. But these qualities are hard to access when we are racing headlong through our days, ruled by to-do lists and timelines. We get brittle. We forget.

In this breathless moment in history, remembering how to *be* is a radical act. If we want our work to spring from wisdom as well as intelligence, we need anchors. Practices. Invitations back to the center.

That's what this section offers: five practices to steady your nervous system, rekindle your imagination, and restore your connection to what truly matters.

For each practice, I've chosen a song. You'll them at www.barbaramcafee.com/full-voice-for-leaders.html. I intentionally use music to slip past the mind and nestle into the body. It lingers where logic cannot. Think about it: many of us learned our ABCs by singing them. Some of you can still rattle off the U.S. states in order because you once sang them to a catchy tune. Let's use that power for something deeper.

Let's begin with the first practice, which correlates with the thumb.

22

PRACTICE ONE: TAME YOUR BRAIN RATS

First listen to this practice's theme song, "Brain Rats," on the website I've already listed.

We all have brain rats.

They're those twitchy little voices that scurry in just when you need steadiness: during a high-stakes meeting, on the brink of a bold move, or in the wee hours when you should be sleeping but instead you're spiraling. They gnaw at your confidence, scamper through your thoughts, and multiply in the dark.

And when you're stepping into something new? Especially with other people watching? That's when they throw a party.

Here are just a few of their greatest hits:

"If people really knew you, they wouldn't like or respect you."

"You're a fraud, and it's only a matter of time before everyone finds out."

"You can't trust anyone."

"Everyone else has it together. What's wrong with *you?*"

Sound familiar?

Many of us assume that this inner commentary is uniquely ours, that we're the only ones playing host to this swarm of self-doubt. But the truth is that most people carry these messages in some form. The details may vary, but the tone is uncannily similar.

So here's the good news: we don't need to exterminate the rats. (Spoiler alert: they're not going anywhere.) But we *can* train them. Like unruly puppies, they can be taught to sit, stay, and stop gnawing on the furniture of your self-worth.

That's the spirit behind my song "Brain Rats." When I first wrote it, I thought it was too ridiculous to share widely. And yet it's become one of my most requested songs. Why? Because it says out loud what so many of us are secretly thinking. And that's the first key to taming your rats:

Say them out loud. Tell someone you trust. Speak the rats into the light. These thoughts thrive on secrecy and shame. They want you to believe that you're uniquely defective, that, to quote the song, "you're the piece of crap around which this whole world revolves." But once spoken, their grip loosens. And often the person you confide in will say something like, "Oh, that one? Yes, I know that voice too."

Another tactic:

Laugh at them. Brain rats love to be taken seriously. Their power depends on your belief in their doom-laced messages. But laughter shrinks them. Humor cuts them down to size. The song does exactly that: it pokes fun at their melodrama until they lose interest and go nibble somewhere else.

When I need inspiration for how to meet hard times with humor, I think of the radiant friendship between His Holiness the Dalai Lama and Archbishop Desmond Tutu. These two extraordinary leaders wisely and tenderly shepherded their people through unthinkable tragedies across many challenging years. Even so, they never lost their capacity to—well—giggle. On my difficult days, I seek out videos of them gently teasing each other and dissolving into joyful chortles. If they can still laugh after all they have seen and endured, perhaps I can, too. They remind me that a strong spiritual practice doesn't just steady us in sorrow: it can keep our hearts light enough to dance.

Feel free to listen to the song one more time. Perhaps you'd like to use your Fire voice to sing along with the chorus: "Brain rats, I've got brain rats—a pestilential blight upon my mind!"

23

PRACTICE TWO: REMEMBER WHY

Now on to our second practice, represented by your pointer finger: remember why.

When you're buried in details and blazing through endless lists, the larger purpose of your work can easily fade from view. It takes conscious intention to stay connected to the *why* behind the myriad *whats* you tackle every day.

People in wisdom traditions across time and cultures have recognized the need for touchstones that jog our memory and bring us back to center. Here's an incomplete but heartfelt list of ways to pause, breathe, and remember why:

Daily meditation, prayer, or chanting. Many people carve out time each morning for this practice. Even a few quiet minutes can anchor you in your deeper intentions and bring a welcome dose of peace. The world won't automatically offer you peace, but it's always available the moment you settle, soften, breathe, and listen. What a gift!

Movement practices such as yoga, tai chi, qigong, or running. I'm partial to long-distance swimming, especially in the rivers and lakes near where I live. When I swim the crawl, my gaze swings from the water's depths to the horizon over and over. And when I roll onto my back and look up into a vast sky . . . delicious. Swimming laps in a pool during winter has its appeal, but it's not quite the same. The rhythm and breath you cultivate in these practices follow you into the rest of your day.

Time in nature. On my daily hikes through the woods near my home, I find deep solace in the changing seasons, encounters with deer, rain falling on leaves, snow crunching under boots, and birds calling from hidden branches. Walking unplugged from human chatter can soothe your nervous system and reconnect you to what matters most.

Symbols or images. Visual reminders can take many forms: a beloved piece of art, a meaningful photograph, a piece of jewelry, even a tattoo. Each glimpse offers a gentle nudge toward your deeper *why*.

Poetry. For me, poetry is a powerful mnemonic for remembering why I do what I do. Finding, or writing, poems that awaken you to your deeper story can be a beautiful quest. They become incantations calling you to stay awake and alive.

One of the poems I use in this way comes from the Chinese poet and philosopher Lao Tzu. It inspired the theme song for this practice. In one of those delightful mysteries of the creative process, I set this ancient Chinese wisdom to music in the style of New Orleans jazz. Go figure.

Here's the poem, with a few tweaks to make it fit with the music I composed:

Always we hope someone else has the answer
Some other place will be better than this
And if we wait around long enough
It will all work out.
This is it.
No one else has the answer
There is no better place than where we are
And even if we don't quite understand how
Everything is just the way it should be
(Do-be-do)
At the center of your being, you have the answer
You know who you are
You know what you want
No need to go outside for better seeing
Rather abide at the center of you
The more you leave it
The less you learn
Search your heart
You will see
The way to do is to be

You can listen to the song here:
www.barbaramcafee.com/full-voice-for-leaders.html.

Feel free to sing along with the chorus—and dance if you dare!

24

PRACTICE THREE: HONOR YOUR LINEAGE

To build a little delicious anticipation, we're going to skip the middle finger for now. Instead, let's turn our attention to the ring finger and the third practice: honor your lineage.

We all come from ancestors who lived through impossible things so that we could have the gift of being alive.

We are also shaped by the teachers, mentors, guides, and fellow travelers who have walked beside us and helped us become who we are.

Remembering that we stand in a long line—that we are carrying life and responsibility for only a brief time—can help us zoom out from the small urgencies of our daily concerns. It can connect us to something much larger and more enduring.

I invite you to pause and make a list of your ancestors, both the ones you're related to by blood and the ones you claim as chosen family or spiritual lineage. Then consider: how might you honor the gifts you've inherited from them in the way you live and lead? Take a few moments to reflect and write.

If any of these people are still living, have you told them what they mean to you? I've sought out these conversations in my own life. Each time, those dear ones were deeply moved to hear how they'd shaped my path. Most of them had no idea.

It's also powerful to remember that one day, we'll hand off what we carry to those coming after us—our children, mentees, colleagues, and the young ones in our communities.

So I invite you to reflect:

Who is following in your footsteps?

What message do you most want to convey to those who follow you?

What words or blessings do you hope they carry in their hearts for the rest of their lives?

What mirrors can you hold up for them in which they can see themselves clearly in all their brilliance and possibility?

Feel free to pause while you list the ones coming after you and consider what you want them to know.

I'll close this practice with a song I wrote for my nephew, Travis, during a time when he was walking through shadows. Our lives have been beautifully intertwined since he was fourteen years old. He's trained in Full Voice, and we love singing together. His children are like my grandchildren, since I don't have kids of my own.

This song was inspired by a luminous interpretation from Daniel Ladinsky of a quote by Hafiz: "I wish that I could show you whenever you are lonely or walking in the dark the Astonishing Light of your Being."

That quote has lived on my office wall for years. One day a melody arrived. And many years later, to my surprise, three verses followed.

Travis lives far away, so this song became a kind of prayer for him during that difficult time. He is thriving these days, thank goodness. Whenever I sing it or invite a group to sing it, I imagine Travis receiving a little burst of joyful energy.

You can find the song at www.barbaramcafee.com/full-voice-for-leaders.html.

Once again, feel free to join in on the chorus. You may also consider singing it for someone who needs this message—including yourself.

PRACTICE FOUR: BE KIND

The fourth practice is simple, and at times the hardest: be kind.

It's linked to the pinky finger: the smallest, but perhaps the most elegant of them all.

Of course, kindness often proves most elusive when it comes to ourselves. Those brain rats always want the last word, don't they?

I used to have a ferociously mean inner voice. It said awful things to me when I dropped an egg on the floor or forgot an appointment. Once I confessed to a friend how cruel my self-talk could be. Her eyes welled with tears as she whispered: "It hurts me to hear such harsh words spoken about someone I love so much."

Whoa. That stopped me in my tracks.

Since then, I've noticed a sweet shift in how I speak to myself when I screw up. Now, instead of unleashing a scolding tirade, I simply sigh and say, "Oh, Babs . . ."

Not many people in my life have ever called me by that nickname, so it's a mystery where it came from. But I'm grateful for its arrival—like a gentle friend taking my hand.

As for extending kindness outward, let's invoke Fred Rogers once again.

Fred devoted his life to seeing and honoring the dignity in every person. One of his daily rituals was swimming laps at his local YMCA. One afternoon as he finished his swim, he approached the young man handing out towels in the locker room. The attendant, recognizing him, said shyly: "Hi, Mister Rogers. I love your show."

Many celebrities would nod politely, say "thank you," and move on. But not Fred.

He paused, water still dripping from his hair, and looked the young man directly in the eyes. Then he asked about his family, his dreams, and his favorite things. For those few minutes, Mister Rogers made that steamy locker room the safest, most important place in the world.

I love this story because it reminds me that who we choose to be in the smallest, most ordinary moments can leave an imprint for a lifetime.

Fred Rogers captured his philosophy this way:

There are three ways to ultimate success.

The first way is to be kind.

The second way is to be kind.

The third way is to be kind.

This practice's theme song is "Such as These." I wrote it after a business trip to Chicago. Though I was cofacilitating an event for a large corporation, the song isn't about my clients. It's about three luminous souls, each doing humble, thankless, often underpaid work, but doing it with grace and dignity:

A woman cleaning a bathroom at the Minneapolis–St. Paul airport, singing her heart out as she worked.

A security guard at the Harold Washington Library who stood in a windowless hallway all day, greeting each person who passed with a warm "hello."

A man with tangled hair and broken glasses, playing exquisite saxophone in a light rain on State Street.

I dedicate this song to all who choose kindness—and who, by doing so, make life infinitely more lovely.

You can listen to the song at www.barbaramcafee.com/full-voice-for-leaders.html.

26

PRACTICE FIVE: COMPOST THE MEANINGLESS

And now the moment you've been waiting for: the fifth and final practice, represented by the middle finger. Yes, the one we sometimes lift high to express rejection.

Because that's exactly what this practice is about: making clear choices about what we're ready to say farewell to.

The great Spanish cellist and activist Pablo Casals once said: "Resist doing things that have no meaning in life."

Of course, I know that many of the things we do are obligatory—at work, at home, and in our communities. People count on us to keep our commitments. I'm not suggesting you give up paying your taxes, picking up your kids from daycare, or bathing regularly. Those things definitely have meaning for life, right?

But as leaders, and as human beings, we often keep adding new responsibilities to our already brimming plates until every moment is packed with urgent activity.

Now and then it's worth asking, "What could I gently—or boldly—take off my plate?"

When I offer this practice in my live keynotes, I invite people to shout out things they're ready to give up. Here's a sampling of what they've said over the years:

- Ironing bedsheets
- Wearing control-top pantyhose
- Ruminating over things that have already happened
- Chasing the perfect career, family, house, body . . . (fill in the blank)
- Complaining about *them*—whoever *they* happen to be
- Scrolling and scrolling social media feeds
- Buying stuff they don't need
- Trying to please everyone all the time
- Dyeing their hair
- Losing those last five or ten pounds

Did anything on this list spark ideas about what you'd like to release? Feel free to jot down your own list.

This practice can also open up some fascinating, and possibly hilarious, conversations with your teammates, family, or friends. You may want to consider inviting them to create and share their own lists.

So there they are: the five practices to sustain your being:

- Tame your brain rats.
- Remember why you do what you do.
- Honor your lineage.
- Be kind to yourself and others.
- Compost the meaningless.

May these practices deepen your connection to your own soul, lighten your burdens, and keep your spirit bright.

May you release what no longer serves you and nourish what truly matters.

And may you remember, always: You are not here merely to do; you are here to *be*. The world needs the fullness of your being.

I'll close these practices with one more song, one full of questions that begin, "What if?" If you listen carefully, you may hear a few more things ready to be composted.

You can listen to it here: www.barbaramcafee.com/full-voice-for-leaders.html.

27

FAREWELL—AND FORWARD

And so, dear traveler, we arrive at the end of the winding path that we've walked together.

We've explored how your voice carries your whole self into the world—your wisdom, your wounds, and your wonder. We've sung songs, whispered secrets, laughed at brain rats, and practiced speaking from the five elements of Earth, Fire, Water, Metal, and Air.

We've remembered that leadership—and life—are not just about *doing* but about *being*.

We've honored where we come from and dreamed of who we might yet become.

And we've dared to imagine that even in these uncertain times, we can choose presence over panic, kindness over cruelty, and meaning over motion.

I hope you leave this book knowing:

That your voice matters.

That your full, true sound belongs in the world.

That you can speak, and live, with clarity, compassion, courage, and joy.

At the beginning of this book, I shared my intention to change the way you think about, and use, your voice forever. So now I ask you, gently and sincerely: have I succeeded?

Take a breath. Let yourself linger here.

I invite you to reflect on these questions not as a checklist, but as a mirror held up to your own growth:

What surprised you along the way? How has your attention to your own voice shifted?

Where have your vocal choices widened, deepened, softened, or brightened?

Are your ears now attuned to the elements swirling in others' voices?

What new leadership possibilities are opening through your voice?

Have you chosen any archetypes to walk beside you?

Have songs or poems begun to live in your body?

What has your voice revealed about who you are becoming?

As we end this book, I offer this blessing to you:

May you continue to discover yourself through the sound of your own voice.

May your voice become a vessel for truth, tenderness, and transformation.

May you speak with flexibility, clarity, power, and pleasure.

May you grow ever more able to meet others heart to heart, voice to voice.

May your leadership flow from the rootedness of Earth, the spark of Fire, the balm of Water, the edge of Metal, and the breath of Air.

May you speak words that heal, connect, and inspire.

May your breath remind you that you are alive—and that your presence is enough.

May you honor your ancestors and bless those who follow.

May you compost what no longer serves you and plant seeds of possibility.

And may your voice, in all its colors and textures, be the music that guides you, and others, home.

Thank you for letting me accompany you on this part of your journey.

Until we meet again, may you dwell in the spirit of *yes*.

As a final benediction, I invite you to listen to one more song: "Yes": www.barbaramcafee.com/full-voice-for-leaders.html.

ACKNOWLEDGMENTS

Thanks to:

My many voice clients, for trusting me with your tender, surprising, and glorious voices over these past three decades.

Full Voice coaches and trainers, for carrying this work into the world in beautiful, nourishing, and surprising ways.

Saule Ryan, for calling forth my voice so many years ago and traveling beside me ever since.

Wise teachers for midwifing my voice: the late Denis Brown, Marilyn Habermas-Scher, Richard Armstrong, Kevin Crawford, Stephen Houtz, and Judi Vinar.

Meg Wheatley, for wise mentorship and faithful friendship over these many years.

Peter Block, for calling my voice more fully into the world.

The late Angeles Arrien, for nourishing insight and clear witness.

Parker Palmer, for abiding wisdom and for coining one of my favorite handles: "a one-woman Burning Man Festival."

Organizational development mentors and colleagues Patrick O'Brien, Susan Rosenthal Kraus, and Marilyn Larson, for catalyzing transformations of all kinds.

Jason Shannon of Zoo School Studio, for recording wizardry and deep friendship.

The team at G&D Media, for bringing this book to life: Gilles Dana, Ellen Goldberg, Evan Litzenblatt, and Meghan Day Healey.

Agent Dan Strutzel, for shepherding the process.

The circle of friends, for holding my heart in your hearts.

The Mississippi and St. Croix Rivers for lifelong teaching and delight.

My ancestors, named and unnamed, who persevered so I could be here.

My extraordinary family, for strength, humor, learning, and love.

And finally, the Great Song, for singing us all to life.

SELECTED BIBLIOGRAPHY

Arrien, Angeles. *The Four-Fold Way: Walking the Paths of the Warrior, Teacher, Healer, and Visionary*. San Francisco: HarperSanFrancisco, 1993.

Barks, Coleman, trans. *The Essential Rumi*. San Francisco: HarperCollins, 1995.

Block, Peter. *Community: A Structure for Belonging*. San Francisco: Berrett-Koehler, 2008.

Blood-Patterson, Peter. *Rise Up Singing: The Group Singing Songbook*. Bethlehem, Pa.: Sing Out Publications, 1988.

Bly, Robert, ed. *The Soul Is Here for Its Own Joy: Sacred Poems from Many Cultures*. Hopewell, N.J.: Ecco, 1995.

Bly, Robert, James Hillman, and Michael Meade, eds. *The Rag and Bone Shop of the Heart: Poems for Men*. New York: Harper Perennial, 1992.

Carol, Shawna. *The Way of Song: A Guide to Freeing the Voice and Sounding the Spirit*. New York: St. Martin's Press, 2003.

DeVore, Kate, and Starr Cookman. *The Voice Book: Caring for, Protecting, and Improving Your Voice*. Chicago: Chicago Review Press, 2009.

Ehrenreich, Barbara. *Dancing in the Streets: A History of Collective Joy*. New York: Metropolitan, 2007.

Goman, Carol Kinsey. *The Nonverbal Advantage: Secrets and Science of Body Language at Work*. San Francisco: Berrett-Koehler, 2008.

Goodchild, Chloe. *The Naked Voice: Transform Your Life through the Power of Sound*. Berkeley, Calif.: North Atlantic, 2015.

Grant-Williams, Renee. *Voice Power: Using Your Voice to Captivate, Persuade, and Command Attention*. New York: American Management Association, 2002.

Hirshfield, Jane, ed. *Women In Praise of the Sacred: Forty-Three Centuries of Spiritual Poetry by Women*. New York: HarperPerennial, 1995.

Jones, Michael. *Artful Leadership: Awakening the Commons of the Imagination*. Orillia, Ontario: Pianoscapes, 2006.

Jourdain, Robert. *Music, the Brain, and Ecstasy: How Music Captures Our Imagination*. New York: HarperPerennial, 1997.

Kahnweiler, Jennifer. *The Introverted Leader: Building on Your Quiet Strength*. San Francisco: Berrett-Koehler, 2009.

Karpf, Anne. *The Human Voice: How This Extraordinary Instrument Reveals Essential Clues about Who We Are*. New York: Bloomsbury, 2006.

Keillor, Garrison, ed. *Good Poems for Hard Times*. New York: Penguin, 1995.

Ladinsky, Daniel, trans. *The Gift: Poems by Hafiz, The Great Sufi Master.* New York: Penguin, 1999.

Leviton, Daniel. *This Is Your Brain on Music: The Science of a Human Obsession.* New York: Penguin, 2006.

———. *The World in Six Songs: How the Musical Brain Created Human Nature.* New York: Penguin, 2008.

Linklater, Kristin. *Freeing the Natural Voice.* Hollywood, Calif.: Quite Specific Media Group, 1976.

Love, Roger, and Donna Frazier. *Set Your Voice Free: How to Get the Singing or Speaking Voice You Want.* New York: Little Brown, 1999.

Mathieu, W.A. *Bridge of Waves: What Music Is and How It Changes the World.* Boston: Shambhala, 2010.

———. *The Listening Book.* Boston: Shambhala, 1991.

———. *The Musical Life: Reflections on What It Is.* Boston: Shambhala, 1994.

McAfee, Barbara. *Full Voice: The Art and Practice of Vocal Presence.* San Francisco: Berrett-Koehler, 2011.

McKnight, John, and Peter Block. *The Abundant Community: Awakening the Power of Families and Neighborhoods.* San Francisco: Berrett-Koehler, 2010.

Montello, Louise. *Essential Musical Intelligence: Using Music as Your Path to Healing, Creativity, and Radiant Wholeness.* Wheaton, Ill.: Quest, 2002.

Oliver, Mary. *New and Selected Poems.* Boston: Beacon, 1992.

Palmer, Parker. *A Hidden Wholeness: The Journey toward an Undivided Life.* San Francisco: Jossey-Bass, 2004.

———. *Let Your Life Speak: Listening for the Voice of Vocation.* San Francisco: Jossey-Bass, 2000.

Ristad, Eloise. *A Soprano on Her Head*. Moab, Utah: Real People Press, 1982.

Sacks, Oliver. *Musicophilia: Tales of Music and the Brain*. Rev. ed. New York: Vintage, 2008.

Senge, Peter. *The Power of Presence*. Audio CD. Louisville, Colo.: Sounds True, 2008.

Senge, Peter, C. Otto Scharmer, Joseph Jaworski, and Betty Sue Flowers. *Presence: Human Purpose and the Field of the Future*. Cambridge, Mass.: Society for Organizational Learning, 2004.

Wheatley, Margaret J. *Restoring Sanity: Practices to Awaken Generosity, Creativity, and Kindness in Ourselves and Our Organizations*. San Francisco: Berrett-Koehler, 2024.

———. *So Far from Home: Lost and Found in Our Brave New World*. San Francisco: Berrett-Koehler, 2012.

———. *Turning to One Another*. San Francisco: Berrett-Koehler, 2002.

———. *Who Do We Choose to Be? Facing Reality, Claiming Leadership, Restoring Sanity*. San Francisco: Berrett-Koehler, 2017.

Whyte, David. *Crossing the Unknown Sea: Work as a Pilgrimage of Identity*. New York: Riverhead, 2001.

———. *The Heart Aroused: Poetry and the Preservation of the Soul in Corporate America*. New York: Currency Doubleday, 2002.

www.ingramcontent.com/pod-product-compliance
Lightning Source LLC
Chambersburg PA
CBHW071234210326
41597CB00016B/2050

* 9 7 8 1 7 2 2 5 0 7 3 8 1 *